The
BEGINNING
Starts at the
END

Caroline Hanna Guirgis

WESTBOW
PRESS®
A DIVISION OF THOMAS NELSON
& ZONDERVAN

WestBow Press books may be ordered through booksellers or by contacting:

WestBow Press
A Division of Thomas Nelson & Zondervan
1663 Liberty Drive
Bloomington, IN 47403
www.westbowpress.com
1 (866) 928-1240

Scripture quotations are from the ESV® Bible (The Holy Bible, English
Standard Version®), copyright © 2001 by Crossway, a publishing ministry
of Good News Publishers. Used by permission. All rights reserved.

ISBN: 978-1-9736-3297-9 (sc)
ISBN: 978-1-9736-3296-2 (hc)
ISBN: 978-1-9736-3298-6 (e)

Library of Congress Control Number: 2018907785

Print information available on the last page.

WestBow Press rev. date: 7/6/2018

To my mother, Aida, with love and affection. No mother should bury her son. Mom, John is not dead. He is alive with Christ in heaven. You pursued John with unswerving love and devotion to rouse him so that he could deal with and heal from drug addiction. You redeemed him from the pit of destruction and set him on the path of construction. You helped John build a new life rooted in Christ. His redemption, restoration, and renewal were part of God's plan for his life. But you were an instrument in the hands of God to author one of the greatest stories written. Thank you for never giving up on John and for sharing your son. John's life is the gift that keeps giving. This book is one of them. Be blessed!

Contents

Part 3: The Beginning

Foreword

It would have been a great read. I wanted to write a book in 2001 after returning from my first missionary trip to Africa. I was inspired by the people I traveled with and the philanthropy work we did. I witnessed faith, hope, and love in action. No matter how hopeless their lives appeared, the Kenyans possessed unwavering faith and joy beyond reason. But the experience that prompted me to write was an encounter I had with God while sitting by Lake Victoria. It was a brisk, cool morning, and my missionary group was scheduled for devotions. I didn't enjoy such quiet moments because I could not harness my thoughts, quiet my mind, and reflect on Bible verses. And I could never hear God speak to me or even feel His presence. While everyone appeared to be relishing the moment and savoring the presence of God, my erratic thoughts were my only companion, and they were disruptive. That particular morning I left everything I needed in my room—my blanket, journal, Bible, and pen. I basically had nothing with me, so I watched the rest of my group reflect, meditate, and pray. They looked peaceful, and I envied their discipline. I tried to follow their example but was distracted by my judgments. I was not living up to biblical morals and standards, so this caused a rift between God and me in my mind and heart. My view of God was through the eyes of religion. Since I wasn't living a true Christian life, I was certain God was angry at me. I sat silently, reflected on the beauty of nature before me and began to wonder about

God. I could not speak words; however, my heart was longing to feel His presence, though I felt impure and unworthy. I fought to channel my thoughts, appease my mind, and rest, but I was struggling to overcome the battles in my mind. Because of the cool temperature, I began to shiver uncontrollably. I did not want to interrupt anyone's quiet time, so I hesitated to ask for a blanket.

Then something strange occurred, so bear with me as I try to describe the experience in words. Seriously, there are no words to accurately describe what I felt in that brief moment. Suddenly, warmth embraced me, and I was no longer shivering. My heart settled, and my thoughts dispersed. Unfathomable peace filled my heart, and I immediately calmed down. I was speechless. My mouth opened, but no words were spoken. I looked around to see if someone wrapped a blanket around me, but no one was near me. I knew at that instant I had encountered God, and it was breathtaking; however, I did not fully grasp it. I could not comprehend what I had experienced. Though my religious background obstructed my view of God and His love for me, I could not wait to write a book and communicate this experience. Even if I didn't believe or understand it, I wanted to encourage others to believe in God and tell them that He does exist. Had I written that book, you would be reading a fairy tale and not the truth. The encounter was real, but my heart was not ready for transparency. The book would have been warped with my own judgments and obscure perspective of God and religion. Despite that beautiful moment, I was too guarded and proud to expose my inner struggles and was not ready to be vulnerable and honest. Though I will never forget that lovely morning at Lake Victoria, I later experienced God more intimately through a series of intense trials and insurmountable struggles. I never expected to write about a tragedy that left me in great despair. Therefore, the composition of this book has been a long, tiresome journey but one that has been life-changing.

This book is about hope shining through the darkness. It

unfolds the story of one of the most influential men in my life, my brother John. From a drug addict to a pastor, John Hanna lived a life of true hope. He overcame his addiction through the gospel of Jesus Christ. Being released from his bondage unleashed a renewed man. He was not ashamed of his past because he knew it was part of God's plan. He was not afraid to be weak because he knew the weary were strengthened. He never cowered from sharing his story because he knew people would be encouraged and God would be glorified. Through his journey John taught me that religion independent of a personal relationship with Jesus Christ was a life devoid of hope. In the face of religion, John identified his addiction as sin, but through a personal relationship with Jesus Christ, the grace of God met him in the dark valley and transformed him. John's redemption and restoration were impactful. It compelled me to share his story to encourage people to never lose hope. His voyage taught me no one was too far gone for God's reach. There was no stronghold, oppression, circumstance, or suffering that cannot be redeemed and restored. When he reached the end of himself, John knew it was the beginning of God working in his life. This sounded good as it applied to my brother's life, and it was inspirational to write about that experience. I desperately wanted to believe this truth, but when faced with life's toughest challenges, I almost lost hope. I felt alone, destitute, and hopeless. How do I have hope in a hopeless situation? It took me thirteen years to write this book because my hopelessness controlled me and left me in great despondency. *The Beginning Starts at the End* was originally written for addicts, but it transformed me more than I expected. I thought I had faith, hope, and love, but I learned I was merely a religious woman trying to be my own God. Imagine writing this book when you've lost hope in God, marriage, people, health, and yourself. Just when I thought I reached the end, I realized it was the beginning.

Part 1
The Beginning

Chapter 1
The Game of Life

A T THE BEGINNING OF MY formative years, life was merely a game. Milton Bradley's Life was a board game I played with my brother and sister. It unleashed our imaginations to create perfect lives for ourselves. During those few hours, our ingenuity created a happy and safe world. We lived freely while enjoying the luxury of perfection. Though the game was created in 1860, it was still relevant to three young children in the 1970s.

John, Jackie, and I played this game daily during the summer months. We were only eight, seven, and six years old, and we were living in an apartment in Staten Island, New York. My parents had emigrated from Egypt in the early 1970s, and they worked hard to provide a comfortable lifestyle for us. They worked long hours and attended graduate school in the evenings. Thankfully, my siblings and I relished our time together. Our most valuable asset was the ability to create innovative ways to play and keep ourselves entertained for eight to ten hours per day. Life was our favorite game because it gave us control to create the perfect life. We shared the same dreams and goals. Most importantly, we desired to experience life together forever.

With that goal in mind, John designed his own version of this board game. His imagination was limitless. He created a game with no struggle, suffering, or death. He envisioned a life lived well in paradise, in perfect harmony. We never grew tired of this game. On other days we pretended to be superheroes. John was Superman, Jackie was Wonder Woman, and I was the Bionic Woman. We spent hours solving the world's problems. It empowered us. But we did not spend all our days playing. We read Judy Blume books, cooked, and watched cartoons, such as *Tom and Jerry*, *Woody Woodpecker*, and *Bugs Bunny*. We also did light schoolwork to challenge our minds, so we played school. Life was good. Actually, it was better than good. Life was perfect. This was our dream life.

This dream evolved into reality for years to come. My hardworking parents were heavily involved in our lives. They were fortunate to have the school come alongside them and play a vital role in our developmental years. Though we enjoyed summer months, we loved our elementary school, which was conveniently situated across the street. The administration understood my family's situation and took a keen interest in us. They provided exceptional care for us. They provided us with a complimentary breakfast at the start of school and a snack to take home at the end of the day.

I was the oldest of the three, so John and Jackie relied heavily on me for everything. During the school day, they requested to see me, seeking some level of security. There were days I spent their recess with each one in their classroom. The administration permitted these visits and began referring to me as "the little mother." Ironically, we were each only one year apart, but I took my responsibility as the oldest sister seriously. The faculty and staff at Public School 35 fostered a nurturing environment for us.

Despite financial struggles, my parents provided for our needs. Family life at home was fun, relaxing, and peaceful. My mother planned weekend outings to baseball games, amusement parks, and beaches. We were New York Yankees fans and drove to the Bronx many times to watch baseball games. We were also Dallas Cowboys fans but didn't travel to Texas for any games. People were surprised we were Dallas fans in New York. The explanation was simple. My father's brother-in-law immigrated before us and wanted to assimilate. During the 1970s, the Dallas Cowboys were known as "America's Team," so he adopted them as his favorite. My father followed suit. And the cheerleaders were easy on the eyes, not that my uncle, father, or brother noticed!

John was passionate about everything, whether it was playing Life or watching sports. He did everything with heart and soul. He was a loyal fan of the Yankees and Cowboys and owned most of their gear. We watched all their games on television, regardless of what Jackie and I wanted to watch. And we watched them as a family because John loved to be surrounded by his family.

We were also privileged to have extended family live nearby. We spent most of our weekends with our cousins playing house, playing outside, and having sleepovers. We treated them like siblings, and the feeling was mutual. We started family traditions, such as Friday night pizza dinners. We had others, but this was our favorite. Growing up in Staten Island taught us to be independent. My parents allowed us to walk to the pizza place on Friday nights to pick up dinner. As we grew older, we were permitted to ride the city bus to the Staten Island ferry and meet my mother in Manhattan for lunch. We were still young, but this prepared us to be bold and live without fear. We were mindful of strangers and did not stray from one another. Experiences such as this strengthened our bond.

Chapter 2
Where It All Began

URING THE LATE 1970S, MORE Egyptians immigrated to New York, and we were soon surrounded by a circle of friends who became part of our family. We were Coptic Christians, and the first few Coptic churches were established in Queens, Brooklyn, and Jersey City. We settled in St. George's Coptic Church in Brooklyn. Our parents appreciated the American culture but felt more comfortable socializing with fellow Egyptian Christians. The Coptic church was not just a place of worship for our family but also an extension of our home. Our church family grew, and our social life revolved around the church and its activities.

My parents went to great lengths to protect us and thought the church would be the safest place. Though they did their best, they could not escape the reality of life. We experienced death for the first time, and it was sad. Our maternal grandmother, who immigrated with us, died of breast cancer in December 1976. We loved her very much. She taught us how to speak Arabic and played hide-and-seek with us. We did not understand death, but we knew she went to heaven, which seemed so far away. John, Jackie, and I witnessed our mother's deterioration for months. She took a leave of absence from work and traveled to Egypt to mourn with her other relatives. My father took care of us during that time. I missed my mother terribly, but John and Jackie bonded with my father. I loved my father but did not form the same connection. When my mother returned from Egypt, she never went back to work. The church family provided her with support and love during that time. Because my grandmother's death left a void in my mother's heart, she engrossed herself in ministry and sought comfort from it.

Soon the church became the center of our lives. My father was worried but wanted to respect my mother's feelings. His primary concern was our spiritual development. He realized our family's interest in the church had nothing to do with God. He understood it filled a void in my mother's life. He further witnessed the church become our playground and country club. It was a sense of belonging to our family.

He loved us enough to give us something deeper, specifically a personal relationship with Jesus Christ. My father revered the church and its rules but wanted to ensure Jesus Christ was the center of our worship. He knew when people abided by rules with their own strength that they did not rely on God. It became his pursuit to infuse us with the Bible. His desire was for his children to build a personal relationship with Jesus Christ. He was mindful of our young minds and inability to understand such an intricate relationship. In his wisdom, he did not thrust God on us. Instead he became a reflection of God's love and exemplified it through the way he lived his life. He was gentle, kind, patient, and joyful in all circumstances and never wavered in his faith.

After dinner every evening, my father read a children's Bible to us and brought the stories to life. He was animated and gifted in capturing our attention for hours. We loved hearing the Bible stories, but they were just bedtime stories to us. At the end of each story, he reminded us that Jesus Christ died for our sins. We were fascinated with stories like Noah's ark, Moses, the Ten Commandments, and the miracle of the five loaves and two fish. We enjoyed hearing about the miracles because they ended happily. He read about the blind man seeing, the lame man walking, Peter walking on water, and Jesus calming the storm. He was captivating and unfolded the stories in the most creative ways so we craved more. Though the crucifixion and resurrection were always a mystery and difficult to digest, he told us about it every night. And we were always confused and asked the same questions. He never grew tired of our inquisitiveness. He actually welcomed it.

We couldn't fathom why Jesus Christ, the Son of God who performed miracles, had to be whipped, beaten, and nailed to a cross to die. It was such a brutal and horrific way to die. Why did Jesus die for our sins? What mistakes have we made? We were still children. What did we do wrong already?

With great patience, my father would start at the beginning— in the garden of Eden, when life on earth was perfect. God created Adam and Eve, placed them in the most beautiful garden, and gave them everything they needed. He forbade them to eat from one tree. That seemed like such a simple command. But was it?

I used to be irate when my father explained they disobeyed and ate from the tree. Without judgment or rebuke, my father used mistakes from our lives to help us understand sin. For example, we were not allowed to play basketball in the apartment. John was not a rule follower, and admittedly, neither was I; however, it took me years to realize that. John was persuasive and convinced me to play with him one day. He threw the ball. I missed it, and we knocked the lamp off the coffee table. We fabricated a story to avoid punishment. This was just one example of many. Though we deserved punishment, we were disciplined with love. Our father wanted us to understand God did the same with Adam and Eve. There had to be consequences for their disobedience. Instead of punishment, God sent His Son to die so mankind could be redeemed, restored, and renewed by God. Jesus Christ restored our broken relationship with God through the cross, and all were forgiven. God invited all people to receive this gift of love. It was up to each person to accept Jesus Christ as their Savior, and this was when he explained the personal relationship with Christ. He encouraged us to open our hearts to receive Jesus

Christ. My father made it clear that God's work was finished and that we didn't need to work our way into heaven. We choose to follow Jesus, and the Holy Spirit becomes our guide and Comforter through life. He further explained the sacraments of the church and the vital role each one played in our spiritual life. It sounded simple, and it instilled a desire within us to choose that path, especially John. He wanted to go wherever my father was going. We continued to listen intently because we loved hearing about the beauty of heaven and the perfect life that awaited us. John, Jackie, and I heard the same message repeatedly from my father, but it later impacted us differently as we grew up. My father spent his evenings in our room, speaking truth and life into our hearts. This was where it all began—in the bedroom we shared in that cozy apartment in Staten Island.

He never grew tired of pouring into us because he knew he had planted seeds that would produce fruit one day. Some evenings our eyelids grew heavy, and our bodies wanted to desperately sleep. But John would always want to hear more. I was convinced John wanted to spend as much time with our father as he could. He loved him dearly and was enthralled by his presence. In our time together, there was endless laughter. When John and my father erupted into laughter, it was contagious, and we laughed until our stomachs ached. He told us funny stories about his coworkers. My father was a conversationalist, and he engaged us in discussing various topics, including current events. At young ages he taught us how to read the *New York Times* and write a report answering who, what, where, when, why, and how. Believe it or not, we looked forward to tackling this challenging assignment. He had the gift of teaching. It was an innate talent.

Because my father exemplified a godly life, he didn't always need to use words, so there were nights we would look out our window and watch people. Our evenings always ended peacefully. There was one evening I will never forget. One night John asked my father, "How do I go to heaven with you, Daddy?"

My father always spoke of his desire to go to heaven. He told us that life on earth was temporary but that we should still live it abundantly. My father placed John on his lap and pointed to his heart. He replied, "God wants you to be in heaven with Him, and that is why He sent His Son, Jesus Christ, to die for your sins. That is called *salvation*. Jesus died so you could live. He saved you. You confess Jesus Christ is Lord of your life and believe it with your heart. Open your heart and ask the Holy Spirit to come live inside you so He may guide you through life. The Holy Spirit is alive and will be your Helper. John, my son. You may not understand this Bible verse now, but one day you will know its depth. The Bible tells us, 'Because, if you confess with your mouth that Jesus is Lord and believe in your heart that God raised him from the dead, you will be saved. For with the heart one believes and is justified, and with the mouth, one confesses and is saved. For the Scripture says, "Everyone who believes in him will not be put to shame"' (Romans 10:9–11). (Romans was John's favorite book in the Bible.) One day we will both be in heaven together."

John smiled and rested his head on my father's chest. Tears welled up in my father's eyes, and I wondered if he was scared John would die before him because he almost did. A few years prior, John was chasing a pigeon on the Staten Island ferry boat and almost fell into the ocean. My father saved him, held him tightly, and told him that he never wanted to lose him. I knew my father's faith was strong, but I often wondered what would happen if John died. Of all the memories etched in my mind, this was one of my favorite because it was a tender moment between a father and a son. It was a beautiful image of a father's love for his child, one I could never forget. I wish our story ended here because it would have been perfect. But it didn't.

Chapter 3
The Move to Middletown

IN 1981, WE MOVED FROM Staten Island, New York, to Middletown, New Jersey. Life became complex, and we began to encounter tough times. Our church life got complicated and it caused tension at home. As mentioned before, the church was the focal point of our life. Therefore, it greatly impacted my family. Though it would be beneficial to share the details of what occurred to help my readers better understand the bearing it had on John, I don't feel disclosing church politics and drama would serve a good purpose. John was a bit apprehensive and sought refuge in my father because he was his safe haven. We were blind to the fact John was not mature enough to handle stress or deal with hardships. His inability to cope was the reason he depended on my father to be his harbor, his escape from reality. I guess some people could say my father was John's drug or outlet. This should have been a red flag. John possessed personality traits that would make addiction more likely. Total dependence was not the only trait John displayed. Ever since he was a young boy in Staten Island, John exhibited impulsive and compulsive behaviors too. Since our parents worked hard to make a living and were not home during the week, I stepped into a role too big for me to fulfill. I could not control his behavior, though I tried. Obviously, I was also too young to detect the issues John was struggling with. He acted out daily, especially after school, and never stopped to think of the consequences he would face. My goal was to resolve the situation before it was exasperated, so I was trained to think and act swiftly. Of course, we can look back and identify the warning signs of addiction, but my parents would have still overlooked them. It wasn't because they weren't good parents, but they were not prepared to face such issues when they immigrated to America. Things were different in Egypt, and even if kids were struggling, it was masked to protect the family's reputation. The upbringing varied greatly and children obeyed out of fear. John was not fearful but was unsettled. Our parents made tough decisions to provide a decent living for us. Their few hours at home were not enough for them to even suspect their son would one day struggle with drug addiction. They didn't have ample time to discipline him effectively. All the signs were there from the beginning but were buried too deep in John for anyone to recognize them. For example, John loved playing and watching sports, which seemed normal. But another trait of an addictive personality was seeking sensations, and John paraded it through his obsession with sports. Again, such behavior patterns appeared normal, so there were no concerns. Most young boys probably possessed the same traits and probably didn't struggle with addiction. But we can't just deduce the roles that trauma and tragedy play in a person's life, which was what happened to John.

As time passed, my father and John's relationship evolved into a friendship built on trust. Because my father made time for John, he confided in him. Our move to New Jersey brought on struggles we were not prepared for. It started with my father's commute which went from a half hour to two hours each way. This changed our evening routine, which John looked forward to. After dinner and Bible study, John and my father talked extensively for hours, but their time was cut short. Despite the extended commute time, my father continued to set time aside for John, but it wasn't enough. He never sought to advance too far in his career as a banker in the World Trade Center, knowing this would have contributed to longer working hours. He made his family a priority and went against the culture where success, status, and money were esteemed highly. His primary concern was to give John the emotional security and safe harbor he needed during his fragile teen years. My father was keen and recognized John's struggles were not limited to one issue. He knew there was something more serious but John couldn't speak of it. It was a few months before John disclosed his deepest pain. My father's dedication set the stage for John to speak candidly about the bullying he was enduring. He gave John the greatest gift a parent can give—his time and undivided attention. My mother resigned from her job when we moved to New Jersey. It was nice to have her home, but she could not shield us from the prejudice we dealt with at school. Middletown residents rejected our Egyptian ethnicity and bullied us. Their anger was fueled by the hostage situation in Iran, which lasted from 1979 to 1981. They were ignorant and didn't differentiate us from the Iranians, so their anger was flared against us. When we walked home from school, boys hid in the bushes and attacked us. They never hit Jackie or me. They beat up John, and it was challenging to fight off three or four of them. Jackie and I tried to help. Sometimes I would shield John with my thin, frail body so he could run and escape the brutal beatings. It was awful, and it traumatized John.

After it was all said and done, we walked home somberly. John was badly bruised and suffered intense pain, but he made us promise not to tell my mother. He hid in his room and changed clothes so that he was wearing long sleeves. Looking back, I realize John was protecting my mother. It was a distressful time for John, and he cried himself to sleep every night. For a long time, he refused to talk about it, even with Jackie and me. Since my father was faithfully present every evening, John finally told him. My father was angry and immediately reported the bullying to the school, but not much was done because the attacks were not on the school property. He was protective of John, and he spent the evenings in John's room, wiping his son's tears and cleaning his wounds. The bullying contributed to John's inner struggles. He could not defend himself. It shattered his self-esteem and robbed him of his confidence. John was not a confrontational person. Nor was he violent. This continued for a long time, and through it all, my father stood by John.

Things didn't improve much when we started junior high school, but the beatings stopped. John, Jackie, and I were fortunate to be in school together, and we definitely depended on one another for support. We made sure we were never alone during lunch, and we enjoyed eating together. But as the years passed, we made friends and were more accepted. The prejudice and bullying impacted John, but he covered up his hurt. Because he had a jovial personality, no one noticed the deep scars. John camouflaged his pain with jokes and laughter. He loved people and never held grudges, so he treated the boys who bullied him nicely. My father knew John was hurting and continued to provide ongoing support and unconditional love. John tried hard to be accepted by his peers. Peer pressure crept up on John, and when he became friends with the boys who bullied him, he got in trouble. They preyed on his vulnerability, knowing John was desperate. He began to dabble with drugs and his willingness to do so gained much favor with these boys. His only restraint was his fear of disappointing my father. He was deeply hurting and couldn't cry on the outside. The only one who heard his silent cry was my father.

They talked every night, and I later learned John told my father about his dabbling with drugs. If it wasn't for my father's presence during these fragile years, John would have been worse off. My father made John feel safe by not overreacting because he started to identify John's addictive personality coupled with his inner struggles. He noticed unhealthy characteristic traits developing in John as he endured bullying and rejection. He addressed them with John, but it was difficult to overcome them without support from school or church. John was labeled as a mischievous troublemaker. Don't get me wrong. John was ill-behaved and definitely caused a ruckus everywhere he went. His mischief was harmless but disruptive. My father was the only one who knew and understood the deep-rooted issues. He wasn't equipped to tackle them, and during the 1980s, Christian counseling wasn't favored. If someone was seeking help on that level, society labeled the individual as crazy. My father wasn't ready for John to be labeled further. My mother loved and adored John but had little tolerance for his nonsense behavior. She was a strict disciplinarian and at times wanted my father to join forces with her. They had different approaches in dealing with John.

Chapter 4
High School Years

THINGS IMPROVED WHEN WE WENT to high school. Not sure how or why it happened, but John became very popular. I have a few ideas, and I believe John compromised his morals and values to be accepted. He never admitted to this, but I am convinced he did more than dabble with drugs. I don't think he was addicted, but I suspected his desire to be accepted forced him to at least pretend. John didn't want to disappoint or shock my father, so he was careful to not get too involved with drugs, alcohol, or sex. John knew at the end of the day, he would give an account to my father. He didn't want to start lying to my father, so he tried hard to stay clear of serious trouble. He grew up to be tall, dark, and handsome, and girls were attracted to him. But he didn't care too much about girls' attention yet. He was strong, so guys knew better than to fight with him or even consider bullying him anymore. John was amusing and often made students laugh, so he spent most of his school days devising pranks. Of course, this caused problems with the administration, but he was more concerned about gaining favor with his peers. He was known for his contagious laughter, which could be heard in the hallways. He had a charming personality coupled with a witty and intelligent sense of humor. He loved to tell jokes, and he laughed until his face turned red. Even if people didn't think the joke was funny, they laughed with John. He was voted class clown, and he considered it an honor. John started to get into a lot of trouble at school, and my parents were contacted by the administration on a daily basis. Whenever something went wrong in a classroom or water fountains exploded, the administration knew John was involved. The vice principal called my father daily at work to report John's misconduct. They became well acquainted, and she respected my father's patience with John, so she tried to work with him. My father talked to John in the evenings and gave him the opportunity to explain his motivations.

My father was not blind to the root of John's issues. He exercised wisdom and patience by pointing John back to the Bible and reminding him of his need for a relationship with God. It was difficult to instill biblical truth in John's mind and heart, but my father knew John was listening. Though most of the mischief was harmless, he still had to be reprimanded. John served the in-school suspension at least once per week. He made everyone laugh and got into more trouble. Jackie and I were known as Hanna's sisters and were associated with him, though we stayed out of trouble. John was brilliant but rarely did his homework. He was more interested in memorizing sports players' statistics. He was advanced two years in some courses, so he and I had classes together. It irritated me when he scored higher on tests because he never studied and barely attended classes. My father did not disregard John's behavioral issues but was proud of his academics when he made an effort because he knew John was smart. He emphasized the importance of school and good behavior but repeatedly told John the root of his problem was his broken relationship with God. He understood how challenging teenage years were, but it did not stop my father from sharing the gospel with John daily. He never gave up or lost hope. He believed in John and had faith one day he would be transformed. My father believed John was going to do amazing things for God one day. He envisioned this for Jackie and me too. He believed that God had a calling on our lives and that our turbulent journeys would lead us to fulfill our divine purpose to further God's kingdom. Quite frankly, this intimidated me because I did not possess my father's spiritual eyes or faith to accept God's plan.

Chapter 5
Daddy's Words

OUR FAMILY DYNAMICS CHANGED DRASTICALLY in the mid-1980s. My mother's brother died of liver cancer, and my parents made a wise decision to become legal guardians of her twin nieces. They were abandoned by their mother at age four when their father was diagnosed with terminal cancer. Our family of five grew into a family of seven. We loved our cousins and were excited to have them move in with us, but of course, there were struggles. I respected my parents for their decision to give Doris and Elizabeth a home and a family. We did our best to help them adjust to their new environment and school. They moved from California to New Jersey, and the culture shock was challenging. With more girls in the house, John and my father spent most of their time together after dinner and Bible study. We continued to commute to church in Brooklyn weekly. It slowly intensified the tension at home, which also affected our family dynamics.

In 1988, tragedy struck our church community, and our families were left distraught and saddened. Our closest friends' father suddenly passed away. There were four kids, and the twin brothers were John's best friends. A few years before their father's death, one of the twins was diagnosed with bone cancer, and this affected John tremendously. We spent most of our weekends with Robert since we knew he was terminal. Our church community

21

prayed for Robert, imploring that God spare his life. We witnessed a few miracles but not enough. John prayed a lot but felt his prayers weren't being answered because Robert's case worsened. Unfortunately, as Robert was fighting for his life, his father died on May 18, 1988, and the tragedy rattled our church and family. His father battled hepatitis but was more concerned with his son's serious health condition. Robert was scheduled for surgery on the day of his father's funeral, so his family asked if I could stay with him. The rest of my family attended the funeral to support Robert's siblings and mother. I commuted with my father by train from Middletown to Manhattan. The commute was two hours, so my father and I had plenty of time to talk. I was disheartened by the tragic death and had questions. I asked my father why God would take Robert's father when Robert needed him. My father explained it was God's plan, and though it made no sense, it was perfect. Death was sorrowful, and there should be time to mourn. The Bible promised to comfort those who mourned. He promised Robert would be comforted by his hope in Christ. I grappled with having hope during such a sad time. My father elucidated that people lose hope when their suffering becomes bigger than God. He did not minimize the loss because he, too, was mourning. It required strong faith to possess such hope.

My father shared his heart with me. He was aware of a secret my mother and I had kept from him. My mother allowed me to *date* Robert's older brother, but it was not accepted in our culture to date, especially at age sixteen. She drove me from Middletown to Brooklyn one Saturday per month to spend time with him. My father was conservative and probably would not have allowed me to date. Even though we were no longer dating, my father had known all along. He was not angry and trusted my mother's decision but needed me to trust him too. It was important to him that I knew this information. I appreciated him for not condemning or lecturing me. I knew he had a more comfortable relationship with John and Jackie. He assured me he loved me just as much and wanted our relationship to evolve into a strong bond. He turned to me and said, "Your picture is the only one I have on my desk at work." I never knew that. He continued, "When I look at your picture throughout the day, it makes me smile. You are going to be a life-changer and will draw many to Christ because you have a special gift. God has a calling on your life." I was taken aback because I was not aware of my father's interest in my life. He had much to tell me and seized the moment. "The Lord gifted you with selfless love, and you demonstrated it in the way you cared for John and Jackie. From a very young age, you put your brother and sister's needs before your own. You will become a godly wife and blessed mother. I will never choose your husband for you because I trust that you will desire a righteous man, one who loves God above all else. He will not be perfect, but his rooted heart in Christ will empower him to love and honor you endlessly. Listen carefully to me, Caroline, and please do not forget my words. You will encounter troubles in your marriage and motherhood because all people are sinners. But do not enter your marriage with divorce as your way out. When you face obstacles, seek to restore your relationship with God first. All struggles stem from a broken relationship with the Lord. As you put on Christ daily, your husband and children will draw nearer to the Lord and will be transformed. Don't change or fix your husband and children, but surrender them to God. Only God, Caroline, only the Lord softens hearts. Keep your eyes on Jesus Christ, and you will never lose hope. If you take your eyes off Him, you will fall into despair. I have been praying for your future husband to love, honor, and cherish you according to the biblical principles. My prayer for your children is for them to live out their faith boldly and proclaim the gospel. Take comfort in knowing your family is already anointed by God to do His work. Remember my words, Caroline."

I was speechless. I was only nineteen years old and did not fully understand the depth of the words imparted to me. I hung onto each word because, despite my youth, I was mindful of my

23

father's wisdom and spiritual strength. He searched my eyes and recognized my desire to heed his advice. He smiled. I did not know how to express my emotions, so my father let his words seep into my mind. My father was sensitive to my sadness for Robert, so he comforted me by saying, "I know you are sad for Robert. I am very sad for him too, especially because he is suffering from a very painful kind of cancer. His father went to heaven and is alive. There is no death in Christ. Heaven is glorious. It is more beautiful than our minds could envision. God will never forsake Robert. Caroline, Jesus Christ is Robert's only hope. He will ease his sufferings, wipe his tears, and prepare his heart to be with him in heaven too. We are all destined to be with God for eternity. There is no suffering on earth that compares to the glory that awaits us in heaven. For now, we love Robert and suffer with him. I know you wanted to attend the funeral, but I am proud of you for thinking of Robert's needs. We don't want him to be alone, so it is sweet of you to be with him."

We still had a half-hour commute, so my father took a nap. I understood why John enjoyed speaking with him. My father was spirit-filled, nonjudgmental, and easy to speak to. One of his greatest attributes was his reliance on the power of God's Word to do its work. He was merely an instrument in God's hand. He never constrained his biblical standards on me. He humbly assumed the role of a spiritual leader and lovingly spoke truth into my life. My father did not question my Orthodox faith (my father was Presbyterian) and respected my decision to follow its teachings. He did not reprimand me for dating without his knowledge. Because my father was gentle, compassionate, and kind, I received his words. He exemplified the love of Christ. My daddy's words became my most cherished treasure. The train pulled into the station, and my father walked me to Sloan Kettering Hospital. My father hugged me and said, "Everything will be fine." He always said, "Everything will be fine."

Chapter 6
The Year 1988

I WAITED FOR ROBERT IN HIS room because he was in surgery for a few more hours longer than I expected. My mind was racing with uncontrollable thoughts while I was alone in the waiting room. John, Jackie, and I never attended a funeral so I was thinking of them and how they were handling the sadness. In our pretend world, no one died, but my father taught me no one died because there was no death in Christ. Maybe our pretend world wasn't imaginary after all. John had the right idea from the beginning. The game of life was not a game after all. It reflected life in heaven, the perfect life. Too bad I was sitting in an oncology waiting room. Life definitely didn't seem perfect at that moment. My thoughts were interrupted, and the nurse informed me that they had wheeled Robert into his room. I composed myself and fought back my tears. As I walked into the room, the nurse moved Robert from the surgical bed to the hospital bed. Robert spent months in that room, and his family did a great job making it cozy. The nurse adjusted his pillow, covered him, and made him comfortable, but he was in pain. A few minutes passed, and he looked at me with droopy eyes and barely said, "My father died, didn't he?" I was caught off guard, so I paused before I responded. The only word that escaped my mouth was, "Why?" I wanted to kick myself for not being swift with a more convincing response.

He fumbled for words and winced. I could not tell if he was sad or in pain, but he continued, "Because he is not here and he is always waiting for me after surgery." And Robert wept. Oh, my heart! I cried because I could not fight back the tears anymore. I reluctantly held him because first, I didn't know how to console him and second, I didn't want to inflict more pain. All I kept saying was how sorry I was. We both cried.

Robert appreciated me being there because he couldn't imagine crying alone. He asked me if his father was in heaven. I responded affirmatively because my father said so and I trusted him. With a feeble voice, he spoke, "Caroline, I will be joining him soon, but I am scared." I did not know what to say. I assured him of God's love and perfect plan for his life.

I invoked him with the same words my father blessed me with. "Keep your eyes on Jesus." Robert grew up in the church but didn't understand God. He promised me he would do his best to seek Christ. Thankfully, his family walked in. When they saw his tears, they knew and ran to embrace him. Even when he was in pain and grieving his father's death, he thought of me and immediately told them I did not tell him the news. He just knew. It was a tough time for the Zakhary family. My family and other close friends piled into the room, and everyone did their best to console Robert. Robert was suffering physical and emotional pain. When I looked over at John, I noticed he was crying in the corner. He was sad for his best friend, and I can confidently say that John was scared to lose Robert too.

One week after the funeral, Robert and Albert (Robert's twin brother) came to stay with us. They were despondent over their father's death and needed to escape home. Robert enjoyed my father's company and loved being with him. My parents loved him but were nervous he would get sick. The chemotherapy compromised his immune system, and he was susceptible to infections. My father gave him instructions daily, and it was well received because he seasoned everything with humor. My father and John were therapeutic for Albert and Robert and kept them entertained. It was May, and the weather was pleasant, so we spent most of our time outdoors. Robert was sad my father was going away on a retreat for Memorial Day weekend. He enjoyed the week with my father and was looking forward to the next one. On the Friday of the long weekend, my father said goodbye, and for the first time since we moved to Middletown, he asked my mother to drive him to the train station. For most people, this would not be an odd request except for the fact that the station was across the street and my father walked it daily. He insisted, and my mother complied. She was gone for a few hours. My father wanted to spend time with her. He reminded her of his deep love for her. Because they handled John differently, my father wanted them to unite to better address John's issues. He further discussed other matters, but his main concern was John. He finally boarded the train. He was leaving directly from work for the retreat with his siblings and their families. When he arrived at work, he called to check in, almost every hour. He reminded Robert to wear sunblock and told him a few jokes on the phone to make him laugh. The calls finally stopped after five o'clock in the evening. We already started to miss him.

The next day the rest of Robert's family and another family came to spend the long weekend with us. We were preparing food and drinks to spend the day at the Jersey Shore. I was tasked with making the iced tea. I put in a lot of ice and stirred it too fast. The thermos exploded. That was around twelve o'clock in the afternoon. Robert's mother and my mother were startled, and they were convinced something terrible had happened. They were being superstitious. My mother was not herself all day. She was filled with melancholy, and I wondered if my father's conversation affected her. She was unusually quiet and disoriented, yet she was willing to go out for Robert's sake. We packed our cars, went to the beach, and had a wonderful time. Robert enjoyed himself, and it made everyone happy. We returned home at midnight, and our friends left except for Albert and Robert. John spent the rest of the evening making us laugh. John was imitating people, and he was very good at it. We were having fun. Then all of a sudden, Robert excitedly pointed to the window and shouted, "John, your dad is here. I guess he decided to come back early." John ran to the door with anticipation until my mother said, "This is not good." She ran after John, pushed him out of the way, opened the door, and stood face-to-face with her brother-in-law. My father's oldest brother stood there for what seemed like an eternity. My extended family stood behind him and appeared too frightened to approach the door. My mother spoke in Arabic as she looked at her brother-in-law. She put her hand up and said, "Do not say it."

She actually screamed it a few times before my uncle said, "I am sorry, Aida." He sobbed and barely pronounced, "Kamal passed away." There was dead silence, and everyone froze in their place. I understood my uncle's words but struggled to accept them. Jackie didn't comprehend Arabic well and nudged me for translation. Jackie was trembling, so she had an idea but needed clarification. She, Doris, and Elizabeth stood closely behind me because they were afraid.

Dazed, I said, "Daddy died." She looked at me, expressionless. Jackie was daddy's little girl. She adored him. Doris and Elizabeth barely recovered from their father's death, so this hit them hard.

Robert looked at John for interpretation, and John replied stoically, "He said my father died." Albert and Robert were in disbelief and retreated to John's room. The foyer cleared, and everyone moved slowly into the living room. John, Jackie, and I continued to stand in the foyer. We looked at one another, and no words were exchanged for a few minutes until John broke the silence, "Daddy didn't die. He is still alive. I know he didn't die. He wouldn't leave us." I desperately wanted to believe him. My mind briefly wandered to the time we played the game of Life where there was no death, cancer, or sorrow. This hurt too much. It hurt so much my heart stung.

My mother collapsed, and my father's family knew she was in shock. John, Jackie, and I could not move. We stood there in disbelief. Albert and Robert emerged from John's room, crying with Doris and Elizabeth in the corner. My uncle was very sad. My aunts and cousins were weeping. Everything seemed surreal. It was midnight, and the news about my father spread widely. My uncle was startled that we hadn't received his earlier message. He tried to alert us prior to his arrival from Pennsylvania. The retreat was in Pennsylvania, so he called our priest to tell him the tragic news. The priest and board members drove a long distance to our home and waited until eight o'clock in the evening. They assumed we were away for the long weekend, so they left. When my uncle arrived, he thought we already heard the tragic news. He was not prepared to be the bearer of such news. He and the rest of the family were perplexed when they heard our laughter through the open windows. They stood outside or some time. Secretly, he was hoping we were already notified so we would have time to let the news seep in. Quite frankly, I don't think the few hours would have made a difference. The hours of the night were elongated. Soon our home was overflowing with people from different walks of life. In spite of my mother's deteriorating condition, she wanted to know the details of my father's death.

My father rode with his sister and niece to the retreat. He was abnormally quiet, but they assumed he was tired. The next morning he had breakfast with the family, but he was pensive and barely spoke. My aunt supposed he was meditating on the gospel message he'd heard the night before. She was worried about him, but when she gazed at him, his face was radiant and exuded peace. After breakfast he told them he would meet them at the tennis courts. My father loved to play tennis. When he returned to his room to get his racquet, he told his roommate, a close family friend, he was having chest pain and to call for his brother. My uncle was a cardiologist. He rushed to my father's room because my father was hospitalized a few months prior for chronic chest pain. After my uncle ran a series of medical tests, my father was discharged. His heart was strong and healthy. My uncle arrived at my father's room and opened the door, and my father was sitting on the chair with his head resting on the headrest. My uncle knew immediately my father had passed away right at that moment. He administered CPR, and my father's roommate dialed 911. The rest of my extended family surrounded the room, praying for a miracle. The news spread throughout the retreat, and everyone prayed. As a cardiologist, my uncle knew my father died, but he relentlessly tried to resuscitate him. My father passed away on May 28, 1988, at 12:00 p.m. Remember that twelve o'clock time? I never forgot it. The time triggered my mother's memory of the iced tea pitcher explosion. She knew something tragic would happen, but she never suspected it would be her husband's death. She told the family about her last conversation with my father. She also remembered his recent extravagant expenses. My father was frugal. However, over the past few months, he bought two brand-new cars, a new lawn mower, and other items. She paused to wonder if my father knew he was going to depart. His actions and conversations alluded to it. My father was spiritual and had an intimate relationship with God, but no one understood the depth. No one slept, and conversations were intermittent. Otherwise, most were silent, still in utter shock. Every so often John walked over to the window, waiting for my father.

Funeral preparations were made without our input. My mother was not able to plan it, so extended family, friends, and the church handled everything. John was angry because he was excluded. John, Jackie, and I weren't permitted to attend the wake. People were concerned we wouldn't be able to handle it. Since we were left behind, we learned of my father's service to others. We were not aware of his extensive ministry because he did it privately. We were a bit surprised but not completely. He was the most Christlike person we knew. His coworkers shared stories that humored us. Apparently, my father was the "work clown." I guess the apple didn't fall far from the tree. It was my father's mission to intermix humor with work, fostering a healthy working environment. His coworkers were sad over his passing. They knew the work environment would never be the same. Schoolteachers and the vice principal visited us too and recounted their conversations with my father regarding John. My father was John's greatest defender, and the administration appreciated his ongoing support. This pained John deeply because he realized his biggest fan was forever gone.

The funeral day arrived sooner than we wanted. It was a somber morning, and the magnitude of sadness in John's eyes was heartbreaking. He walked aimlessly, pacing back and forth from his room to my parents' room. My mother and I needed to collect important items from my father's workplace before the funeral. His coworker accompanied us. The car ride from New Jersey to New York was long and quiet. My mother wept the whole way and did not speak a word. I sat in the back seat and stared out the window. My mind was flooded with memories of my dad's last words. When we arrived at the World Trade Center, I remembered the last time I was there. I had gone with my parents to my father's Christmas party. He and I danced together and realized we would need lessons before I got married. The happy memory faded into a sad image. My father was not going to be at my wedding. We walked into his office, and I noticed the photo my father had spoken fondly of. I held it to my chest and remembered his words. I never told anyone of my conversation with my father. My mother looked at me. "You always thought your father loved John and Jackie more than you. I still remember the day he held you in the hospital when you were born. He could not believe how beautiful you were. He was mesmerized by your piercing blue eyes, jet-black hair, and fair complexion because it did not run in our family. He thought you were the most beautiful baby he had ever seen. As you grew, he respected the way you loved and cared for John and Jackie. He always said you were a gift from God."

When we arrived at the church, my mother could barely walk without any support. She was escorted to the front pew and sat with my father's extended family. John was also in the front pew and stared blankly at the altar. He could not be consoled. The funeral procession began, and melancholy church hymns were chanted. The sadness was gut-wrenching, and the anguish was insufferable. As the casket passed our pews, we all sobbed. The funeral lasted two hours. I still remember one of the priest's words to my mother. Father John later became my father-in-law, but I met his son a few years after my father passed. Father John and his wife knew my family well. Since we were one of the first Coptic families to immigrate, we were well known among the tight-knit Egyptian community.

Father John looked at my mother. "Aida", he said. "Aida, listen to me, my precious daughter, Kamal is in heaven. Rejoice! Kamal is in heaven. He is not in this casket. He is with the Lord Jesus Christ. Let us rejoice on this day and give thanks to God." My mother was looking directly at him, but the words did not resonate with her. She was dazed. More priests, family, and friends shared about my father and we learned more about his compassion, selfless love and wisdom. He was highly esteemed by all. As the pallbearers carried the casket to the hearse, the church was deafened by a shrieking scream. Everyone stopped and looked in the direction where it came from. Amidst such harried commotion, I pushed through the crowd because I knew it was John. He refused to release the casket. He embraced it tightly and wouldn't move. He was tall and strong, and none of the men were able to move him. I begged them to leave him. He drenched the casket with his tears and cried, "*Ya baba*," which meant *father* in Arabic. I pushed some of the men off of him. As they backed off, John cried, "Ya baba, please don't leave me. Please don't go. Please, ya baba, don't leave me. I need you. I love you. I can't live without you." Even as I write these words, I remember his pitiful petition mingled with deep sorrow. Finally, I peeled John off the casket and held him back as they carried the casket away.

My mother, John, Jackie, and I rode in the limousine. Thankfully, the extended family rode with us because Jackie and I couldn't handle my mother and John. We drove away and followed the hearse to the cemetery. It was the longest ride of my life. My mother and John's conditions deteriorated in the limousine, so we stayed in the car at the cemetery. John lost complete control when he saw the casket descend into the ground. John knew this was the end for him. Albert and Robert rode in the limousine with us to be with John. Shortly after, Robert also passed away, and it further devastated John.

Part 2
The End

Chapter 7
College Years

A FEW WEEKS AFTER THE FUNERAL, John graduated high school. It was an emotional day since my father's death still stung. The vice principal exempted John from his final exams. She was mindful of John's brokenness. John was grateful because he could not focus on school. The summer months were harrowing, but we were fortunate to have visitors. If we had no visitors, my mother stayed in her room, and John lay on the couch all day. Jackie, Doris, Elizabeth, and I got summer jobs to help with finances. She had five teenagers to provide for and had been out of the workforce for many years. In addition, she was not in any condition to seek employment. Jackie and I worked together at Friendly's. Doris and Elizabeth worked at Pathmark, a supermarket in Middletown. When we were not working, we frequented the Jersey Shore. We mostly enjoyed our beach trips except for one horrid day.

We went to Asbury Park Beach with family friends. A few of us broke off from the group and took a walk on the boardwalk. We walked into an arcade and were greeted by flirtatious young men who were immediately drawn to Doris. Though she did not reciprocate, their girlfriends pounced on us. Before we knew it, we were in the midst of an unsought brawl. We were not prepared to fight. Doris was swift on her feet and escaped the ferocious poundings. My friend and I were terribly beaten. By the time Doris returned with our family friends and police, we were distraught. Unfortunately, the police did not follow proper protocol in order to avoid racial issues. There were ongoing racial concerns at that arcade, so the police advised us to walk away. We were angry, but we evacuated the beach, licking our wounds. When we returned home, my mother and John were shocked after they saw my bruises. John was furious and wanted to retaliate. He was persuaded not to. John never retaliated his brutal bullying but was not going to let anyone hurt his family. After we slept, John and a few of his friends returned to the beach and avenged me. They did not strike the girls, but they fought the young men. It was not a pretty sight, and they also demolished the arcade. When the police arrived at the scene, John was indifferent but retorted with the same message they delivered earlier. As he walked away, he turned to the nonplussed crowd. "No one hurts my sister and gets away with it!" I never condoned violence, but I was touched that my brother had fought this battle for me.

Summer ended. John and I moved into our college apartment, and we were eager to start a new chapter in our lives. Though John deteriorated throughout the summer and was inconsolable, he was looking forward to this new season in his life. He was glad we were in it together. I encouraged him to attend classes, study hard, and make friends. We started off well, but he quickly declined. One month into college, John skipped classes and spent most of his days in the cafeteria. His idle times led him astray, and he befriended fraternity brothers who smoked weed all day. Marijuana calmed John, and the daily high eased his pain. Or so John thought. He was not prepared for the journey this one drug was going to take him on. At the time, I was not yet aware of his drug problem. I was more concerned about him skipping classes. When we drove back to our apartment, we had dinner and discussed our days. It was obvious John was indolent, but I attributed that to him not overcoming his grief. He constantly reminisced about our father. Our evening conversations were centered on childhood memories. John could not move on.

We began to encounter serious problems when John and his new friends hid drugs in the apartment. I started to work part-time at an insurance company to help my mother with our bills. I went to work after classes, so I returned home after everyone vacated our place. By the time I got home, John and I ate dinner, and he continued to speak about my father. I pleaded with John to attend classes and get a job, but he quickly dismissed my imprudent suggestions. Erroneously, I covered up for John. He made empty promises, and I wanted to believe him. As a result, I gave him too many chances. I always had a soft spot for him. I knew we were getting into deeper trouble when John disappeared for a couple of nights at a time. I was terrified and would search for him. I was not concerned about my safety, though I had a few scares. Most of the time, I returned without John and hoped for the best. When he would finally come home in the middle of the night, he was loud, which disrupted my sleep. It became more difficult to attend classes and work long hours. We profusely argued about him missing classes. His attitude and demeanor changed temporarily to appease me, but it was an interminable cycle. Things quickly spun out of control because John became careless.

One day while sitting in economics class, I saw the school security outside my classroom. I knew something was wrong. As class ended, I ran out to avoid them. They asked the professor for "Caroline Hanna," and he pointed at me. They caught up with me and told me they wanted to search my car. At the time I did not know my rights and did not question them about a search warrant. They escorted me to my car, which John parked illegally on campus. They searched the car for a half hour. They did not find anything, but they fined me for parking illegally. Our parking fines were astronomical, and I could barely afford to pay them. They interrogated me about John's whereabouts, and I told them I did not know. They gave me their contact information. I looked for John frantically without much success. A few hours later, John returned to the apartment. I told him the security guards searched our car and fined us for parking illegally. John was apathetic. We ate dinner, and I continued to probe him because I knew he was in trouble. He did not wince. I confronted him about drugs, but he denied it, which irked me. He admitted he was not attending classes and lost his backpack. John showed no concern and shifted the conversation back to our father. John was an animated and humorous storyteller until grief became the theme of his memories. His laughter was intermingled with tears. His melancholy tone evoked emotions I could not cope with. John could not be consoled and cried himself to sleep every night.

One night I heard John scream. I was startled and ran to his room. He was in a fetal position and shaking uncontrollably. I shook him until he woke up. He sat up and stared at me. He told me he could not live without our father and that he dreamed of him every night. John wanted to die. John was spiraling downhill and was self-destructive. I encouraged him with my father's words that he would one day do something amazing for God. I struggled to believe it but wanted to give John hope. His deterioration was painful, and his life looked bleak and hopeless. Each day we faced tougher hurdles to overcome. Drugs lowered his awareness, and he was forgetful, careless, and neglectful. One day the police showed up unannounced at the apartment. John knew why they came, so he begged me to help him hide the marijuana. I was sick to my stomach. I did not want John to get arrested, so I foolishly helped him. He wrapped up the plastic bag of weed in paper towels and threw it in the toilet bowl. The police searched the apartment. When they entered the bathroom, John and I struggled to remain composed. Oddly, they did not look in the toilet. After the search, they berated John. They were more interested in the drug dealers John was working with. They verbally warned him and made it clear they were watching him. After they left, I yelled at John. He remained calm and promised he had everything under control.

John admitted he was scared. He remembered going to jail for a few hours. When he was in high school, he was taken down to the Middletown precinct for a minor offense. He and his high school friend were throwing snowballs from our house across the street. They were not aiming at anyone, but they hit a detective's car. The detective often got his haircut at the barbershop across the street from our house. Over the years he was exposed to John's mischief. He looked over at our house and knew John threw the snowball. John crouched down on our front porch. He thought he was sly until he saw the detective standing over him. The detective handcuffed John and his friend. The friend slipped out of the car. John laughed. The detective smirked, but he was on a mission. He wanted to teach them a valuable lesson. Jackie and I were instructed to have our mother call the station for John to be released. John did not want to face my mother's wrath, so he begged me to call. He pleaded with his eyes. I bailed him out. My hands shook as I called and pretended to be my mother, but John was home before my mother. After hearing John reflect on that day, I knew I was an enabler. And I did not know how to stop. He paused and looked remorsefully at me. "Caroline, you never gave up on me. You were always there." He promised he would make me proud one day. That day could not come soon enough.

I was also John's advocate in high school. There was one time he was suspended for putting crazy glue on all his classroom doors. John was advanced in math, so we were always in the same math class. One day he was not in calculus class when we were having a test. I knew he was in school because we walked together. I went to the office, searching for him. They told me he had in-school suspension for the rest of the day. I persuaded the supervising teacher to let me visit with John. John was distressed because he was in serious trouble. He told me what he did, and all I thought was, "*Oh, boy!*" He had damaged the doors, and the expense was hefty. As I was talking to him, the vice principal, who became well acquainted with John and my father, flounced into the classroom. At first glance I could tell she had not brushed her hair. She looked disheveled, which was unusual for her. Her hands were shaking, and she was yelling at John. I could not decipher the words, but her body language expressed anger. John was focused more on her odd appearance. She approached John and tripped over another student's backpack. She did not fall, but it almost made John laugh. Things like that made him laugh. Her uncombed hair flipped strangely every time she shook her head. I knew John wanted to laugh, but I made eye contact with him and begged him not to. He understood, so he lowered his head. She demanded that he make eye contact. I knew we were in trouble. When John erupted in laughter, he was unstoppable. To some people, it was annoying, but to most, it was amusing. His laughter was contagious. When John laughed, everyone in the classroom, including the teacher stifled their laughter. This vice principal was respected, but she intimated faculty and students. John was in deeper trouble. I had no idea how the next few minutes were going to unfold. The awkward silence in the room was broken by the vice principal's laughter. Everyone was bemused. She pulled up a desk, faced John, and calmly spoke, "Mr. Hanna, no student in my entire career made me cry more than you, yet no student made me laugh more than you." Definitely not what I expected! She further told him he would serve two weeks out-of-school suspension. John wiped the smile off his face, and his countenance immediately changed. He knew the punishment at home would be more severe than school. The vice principal highly respected Jackie and me. She often told me she could not comprehend how we were John's siblings. John was misunderstood. He was a far better person than people pegged him. I asked if I could intervene on John's behalf. We spoke outside the classroom, and I persuaded her to let John serve the in-school suspension and add chores. She appreciated the chores suggestion and reversed her decision.

John never forgot that incident. My father told John later that evening he admired my courage to plead his case and resolve situations before they exasperated. My father appreciated my intervention because it calmed the situation. I became part of the solution and not the problem. He told John I mastered a life skill most adults struggled to learn. He understood I was young and immature, but he was confident I was going to grow in wisdom. John echoed my father's sentiments. I was petrified when John told me he sought refuge in me. I did not want to be John's safe haven. I was afraid to hurt him because I was not equipped to properly guide him. Alas, nothing prepared me for the challenges we eventually faced. John spent the rest of the evening reflecting on more memories. It was getting dark, and we ate soup for dinner. His fraternity brothers finished the groceries I bought, and I had no money until my next paycheck. John felt bad and apologized for the imposition. He knew it was too much for me to bear. He was hurting, and until he healed, he was going to hurt me again. We found chocolate chip cookies and enjoyed them while watching *Three's Company*. He fell asleep on the couch. My heart was heavy for John because I knew his journey was going to be tumultuous. I went to my bedroom, sat on my bed, and sobbed. I cried because the memories made me ache for my father. His last words to me were so comforting, and I wanted him to tell me that everything was going to be fine. I cried because John was suffering, and I could not save him. I wept because we had no money and I did not know how we were going to survive the upcoming week. I had no one to talk to and felt alone. Where was the God my father talked about in our Staten Island bedroom, the miracle worker? He seemed so distant. I was in my infantile spiritual stage and had a distorted view of God. To me and probably to most people God was a magician. He was supposed to magically make everything better. Instead things were progressively getting worse.

Once again, John's scream pierced the silence of the night, and I frantically ran into his room. He was yelling, "No, ya baba, no." It took me time to wake him up. He sat up on his bed and was startled to see me. He asked me, "Where did baba go?" I taciturnly told him that Daddy had died. He nodded no and said our father was talking to him. I was not a psychologist, but I recognized John's dire need for help. He said my father told him he loved him and that he should put all his hope in Jesus Christ. He promised John that God loves him and will never leave him. John asked my father why he left him. My father vanished, and John screamed. John told me he was going crazy. He finally settled down and went back to sleep. I cried out to God, "Why did you take my father when you knew John would suffer this much? How could the same loving God my father preached about hurt my family so much?" I wanted an answer, but there was only silence. I finally went back to sleep. We both overslept for our classes. John did not even attempt to make an effort, so I left without him. I barely made it to my English class, and the professor glanced sternly at me. The class started to write their essays, and I worked hard to complete mine before it was my turn to read it aloud. After class, the professor asked me if I was depressed. I never experienced depression and was not aware of its symptoms. He told me my last few essays were sad. I fought back my tears, embraced my strength, and told him my father had died and my brother was struggling with his death. The professor suggested I meet with a counselor. I did not have the time then. Nor did I understand the concept of counseling. Instead I went into survival mode. I barely attended classes because I spent most of the days searching for John. We were both placed on academic probation. I was a thriving student and took pride in my school work, but it was no longer important. John's life took precedence. John was getting in trouble with the police almost daily. They never had enough evidence to arrest him, but they knew he was involved in drug trafficking. They were more interested in the people John was working with. They were hoping John would lead them to those people. John was loyal, but he also feared for his life. The dealers were dangerous and threatened to break his legs if he betrayed them. I, too, feared for my life and called for a police escort every time I left the apartment. I definitely kept the police busy, but they understood my trepidation.

When the semester was over, we moved back home. Things

back at home were not going well. Our family was fractured, but we were too broken to recognize our despair. Summer was long, dreary, and sad. We managed to go on vacation to Florida, and we enjoyed our time away. It was the first time John laughed, enjoyed food again, and loved being with family. When our vacation ended, we faced reality again. We had summer jobs except for John. He spent his days on the couch, and this frustrated my mother. He was not helping with any of the house chores, and this aggravated my mother more. I never told my mother John smoked marijuana at college because I thought he had stopped. Back at college, he was getting it from his fraternity brothers but I never suspected anyone in our hometown would be selling pot. I didn't think any of John's high school friends did, so I thought he was safe. I started to suspect he was using drugs when he had bursts of energy followed by long hours of sleep. But like any addict, John denied it and told me he was just depressed. John's demeanor and disposition gradually changed, and I no longer recognized him. His lifeless eyes showed no emotions, and oftentimes he looked through me. His effervescent laughter was muted. I did not think a person could sleep so many hours in one day, but John did. If he was not sleeping, he was eating excessively. He was not socializing much and spent most of his time in his bedroom. His conversations were centered on my father, and I knew this hurt my mother. She was sad for John and felt helpless. As time passed, John withdrew completely and became a loner. He only enjoyed being with my father's family, but their presence made him long for my father more. It triggered painful memories for him. His grief dragged from one year to the next, and it affected our family dynamics. To be fair, we each retreated within ourselves. We masked our pain and moved on.

Chapter 8
Blended Family

A FEW YEARS AFTER MY FATHER passed away, the priest from St. Mark Coptic Church in Jersey City introduced my mother to a single orthopedic surgeon who had three young children. They started courting for a brief period of time before my mother told John, Jackie, and me. My sister and I understood my mother's situation and were mature enough to realize she needed companionship. John did not react the same way. He refused to entertain the idea of my mother getting remarried. Reluctantly, he attended my mother's wedding, and our blended family went on a cruise to celebrate the new marital relationship. We had fun on the Caribbean cruise and became acquainted with our much younger stepsiblings. Reality hit John hard when we returned from vacation, and he escaped. He moved to Florida to live with my maternal uncle. My uncle loved John. He even named his son after him. I stayed in touch with John while he was in Florida. I lived alone in our family home in Middletown. Jackie was away at college, and the twins were living on their own. My mother moved in with her new husband and his children. I visited them often. John assured me he was doing well, earning an income, making friends, and attending church. It was a small glimpse of hope. He forgot to mention he was smoking pot daily. John's situation in

Florida changed. He and my uncle mutually agreed it would be better for John to move back to New Jersey.

John was excited to live with me again. For the most part, we had a blast. During the 1990s when the Dallas Cowboys were in a few Super Bowls, we threw the biggest parties. We knew how to throw parties. I worked part-time at Lord & Taylor and encouraged John to get a job. I also needed him to help out around the house. Initially, he complied, and things were peaceful. Then John reconnected with his friends in Middletown. At first, I was happy for him until our home became drug central station. It took me time to realize it because I was at work most of the day. John and his friend drove me to work because we only had one car. They barely picked me up on time because the drugs fogged their minds. On my days off, I hung out with John and his friends, but they discreetly hid the drugs from me. I knew John's friends were wealthy, but I could not understand how they were not employed. They were fun to have around, especially after living alone for one year. I enjoyed their company, but they were irresponsible and broke some of our appliances. Our washer and dryer broke. John and I dragged bags of laundry to the Laundromat and spent hours washing our clothes. The long hours gave us time to talk, eat, and laugh. John stripped down to his boxers to wash the clothes he was wearing. It definitely drew unwanted attention. When his friends stopped by to keep us company, they were amused. Because they were immature, they thought it would be funny if they washed their clothes. Before I knew it, I was sitting in a Laundromat with a few guys stripped down to their boxers. We ran out of quarters because we used the change to buy all the food in the vending machines. I felt like I was on a *Seinfeld* episode.

His friends were using our house as their second home, but no one maintained it. There were days I forced them to clean up after their mess. They submitted most of the time. I began to worry when the police started to lurk around my home. It triggered memories from when John and I lived in the apartment. The police parked across the street and watched our home from the barbershop. John, Jackie, and I spent many summer days at the barbershop. We trusted Ode, the barber. He gave us lollipops and told us stories. After the police left his shop, I ran across the street to question him about their visit. He was honest and told me they were watching John because he was involved with dangerous drug dealers. I was overcome with fear. When John and his friends came home after being out for hours, I sent all his friends home. He was angry at first, but he knew I was distressed. I confronted him, but John was savvy, sly, and sneaky. I knew he was lying. He appeared normal, but then again, I did not know what normal was anymore. He masked his fear and concern but spent the afternoon in his room. A few of his friends joined him. His friends were usually friendly but were distant and preoccupied for a few days. John and his friends were not just taking drugs. They were also distributing for precarious drug dealers. I had a few scary nights at home when John was out. One night I was walking from the sunroom to the kitchen and saw a dark figure on the deck. I had no way of reaching John, so I called the police. I knew it was not a good idea, but I was terrified. The guy jumped off the deck and ran. I watched him run off and was able to show the police which direction he ran.

The police could not find him, but they warned me that John was dealing with risky men. John was afraid when he saw the police in the driveway. They warned John, and he was scared. He did not know much about the dealers and promised he would stop working with them. He tried to stop dealing with them, but it was not easy. They wanted the money John and his friends owed them. They also wanted them to continue selling drugs for them. John told me it would be better if I went away for a few weeks and stayed with Jackie. So I did, but I knew I was being followed. I was petrified. After a few weeks, John and I returned home and were greeted by a strange man on our front porch. John did not recognize him. He warned John to never call the police again. The drug dealers were angry. We were both scared and notified the police anyway.

They watched our home. I felt protected, but I was frustrated with John and his carelessness. We avoided being home as much as possible and discouraged my mother from visiting. John spent most of his days at friends' houses, and I worked more shifts at Lord and Taylor. Though John was scared, he continued to take drugs. I could not understand what it would take for John to learn a valuable lesson from the mess he created. In his mind, he could not function without getting high daily. I knew he was not just smoking marijuana, but I had no idea what other drugs he was taking. He was shaky, moody, lethargic, and anxious most of the time. He had a ravenous appetite, and he was gaining weight. One night John was nervous and paranoid. He ran through the house, locked all the doors, shut the blinds, and turned off the lights. The drug dealers had been arrested, and he was scared for our lives. John was parading me into a world I did not want to be a part of. The arrest motivated John to make drastic changes. He woke up the next morning and got a job with his friend's father's company. John made positive and healthy changes. He worked daily, ate healthier, and came home every night. He was more engaging and helpful around the house. He paid to fix the washer and dryer. He bought groceries and cooked dinner. John also agreed to start visiting my mother and stepfamily in Staten Island. The visits were pleasant, and John took great strides toward living peacefully with our blended family. He grew to love our stepbrothers, Joey and Christian. He told me he wanted to invest more time in them. I thought it was healthy for John to be surrounded by family and friends. He looked healthier and overall better. I was excited about John's new life. Things improved for some time. I thought that our nightmare was over and that John had overcome his drug addiction. Sadly, John was not drug-free. He temporarily stopped cocaine and heroin, but he smoked marijuana daily. After a few months, the happy days ended abruptly. He declined rapidly. He lost his job.

His friends started coming around again, and they stayed all day. When I came home from a long shift at work, the house was a mess. His friends spent the nights and neglected to lock the front door. Middletown was a safe small town, but because of John's connection with certain drug dealers, I lived in fear. It did not feel safe anymore, so I insisted we lock all doors and windows. John was distracted, so he was not aware of his surroundings. There were a few good days, and I enjoyed the full house when they were drug-free. They played cards, told jokes, ate, and laughed. There were nights when they were drunk and heavily drugged. Those were long nights. I endured it for a long time, but I was depleted of energy. I could not handle John on my own. He was in dire need of professional help. It had been four long years. Ever since I was a child, I had never told on John, but I knew he was in trouble. This was not us playing basketball in the apartment and breaking a lamp. John was a heavy drug addict. My threats never scared John because I rarely followed through. Jackie moved back home after college, and he promised things would improve. He was not a child anymore, but he kept looking back at our childhood years and wanted to go back to playing Life again. John was hurting, and he craved our childhood days. I needed him to grow up and live a better life.

John and Jackie started going out for long nights. They hung out at the clubs at the Jersey Shore with their friends. Jackie knew her limits and was able to set boundaries. She was more willing to go the extra mile with John. He knew better than to invite me on his crazy outings. John appreciated my stance and understood the different relationships he had with Jackie and me. Jackie was not aware of John's serious addiction. She also made a conscious decision to distance herself from all family drama; she sensibly set boundaries. I admired her determination to pursue a healthy lifestyle. At times, it frustrated John. Jackie appreciated John's sense of humor but had a low tolerance for his nonsense. No one put John back in his place better than Jackie. John desired tough love and gave few people permission to exercise it. Jackie was one of those people. John's demeanor continued to change, and I was getting more worried. He got into financial trouble, and I borrowed money from a good friend to pay off John's debt. I knew this could not continue. I finally took the bold step and reached out to my mother. I told her John wasn't doing well. She was already aware of the change in his behavior. However, their relationship was strained because of her remarriage. Nonetheless, she never suspected John was on drugs. Like most conservative Christians, she mistakenly thought we were exempt from such issues. As she spent more time with John, she overcame her denial and faced reality. It was a harsh realization, but she was left with no choice but to tackle the situation.

Chapter 9
New Season

I GOT MARRIED IN MAY 1994. It was a bittersweet day. I longed for my father, but I was marrying a man I loved. My father trusted me to choose my husband and not have a prearranged marriage. Since I was sixteen years old, men asked for my hand in marriage, but my father turned them away. The already emotional day heightened when John was nowhere to be found. John was supposed to give me away. He claimed he had a baseball game, but he disappeared for too long. I knew John struggled with filling in for my father and was overwhelmed. He finally showed up before the limousine was ready to leave. I was angry at John. I desperately wanted to hear my daddy's words again. "Everything will be fine." We finally left for Queens. John rode in the limousine with the bridesmaids and me. He was entertaining as usual, and my friends loved having him in the car. We arrived fifteen minutes early, which was good since my father-in-law was one of the Coptic priests officiating the wedding and being prompt was of extreme importance to him. Everyone got out of the limousine except John and me. For fifteen minutes John ushered me into a different realm. His disposition changed, and he reminded me of my father. It gave me a glimpse of hope. I will never forget John's words on my wedding day. He said, "Caroline, you are getting married today. Wow!" John knew I did not like my wedding dress or veil. I was fine with my mother choosing my gown because at the time we were dealing with bigger issues. Despite that, John told me I looked beautiful. But the words that followed were the ones that left a mark on my heart.

"Caroline, I know some people did not think Mark was the right husband for you. It was hard for you to go against them and follow your heart. You and Mark fasted and prayed and knew it was God's will. That's admirable. God will bless your marriage, so don't ever think you made the wrong decision. Daddy would be proud you chose a godly man. You did not pursue a wealthy man but one who fears and reveres God. Mark has a heart for the Lord. He will build your marriage on Christ, and no matter what you face, your marriage will never fail. Remember, a perfect marriage is two imperfect people who never give up on each other. Daddy always said to make Jesus Christ the foundation of marriage, and you wisely chose the right man to honor Daddy's words. Mark will make mistakes, but a righteous man is not a perfect man. A righteous man is one who chooses to do what's right before God. Mark is a good man, Caroline. He loves you and your family. He never judged me. He never belittled me. You know, once you walk down that aisle, you are making a covenant with God. If you can't make that promise to God, then don't get out of the car. Don't worry about what people will say. Remember, Daddy said marriage was the hardest relationship, but it's not just you and Mark anymore. It will be God, Mark, and you. God will always help you. Just do what Daddy said and keep your eyes on Jesus Christ."

John's words gratified me, and I needed a few minutes to digest them. John saw the hesitation in my eyes. John's perception never ceased to amaze me. I was anxious and nervous. I knew once I walked down the aisle, I was making a covenant with God. I never made such a commitment, so I was apprehensive. John looked at me and said, "I know I am younger than you. But Caroline, I love you more than you know. I know you don't need my approval, but since I am giving you away, you have my blessing to marry Mark and become Mrs. Caroline Guirgis. Let's do this." John and I fought back our tears. I could not believe the words John spoke, and I knew at that moment John would become the man my father was … or even better. John was going to become the man God created him to be. No one could turn such an emotional moment into a humorous one like John. After speaking such affectionate words, John realized he had no idea how to give me away. We laughed until our stomachs ached. The chauffeur opened the door. John stepped out and looked at me helplessly, seeking guidance from me. I asked him to lift my dress off the floor, but I never thought he would expose my entire back. I felt the wind go up my dress and realized what John did. We both looked at each other and gasped, so he immediately dropped my gown. He escorted me to the church entrance. We were greeted by a sea of people who helped John fulfill his role as the brother of the bride. In the Coptic church, the bride and groom walk down the aisle. so John was a bit relieved to hand me over to Mark. John moved into his role as a groomsman. After the honeymoon Mark and I relocated to Virginia for his new job.

After I moved and settled in Virginia, John's life deteriorated. He called me daily to update me on his worsening condition. His calls were like clockwork. I was losing hope for John. We talked through it and he made empty promises. He borrowed a lot of money from me. Though hope was slowly fading away, I could not give up on my brother. It pierced my heart to ask my husband to help my drug-addicted brother, but Mark always helped out. John appreciated Mark more for getting him out of trouble. My mother became keenly aware of John's struggle and started to focus intently on him. She monitored him, called him, and fought to keep him out of trouble. John was arrested and spent many nights in jail. She bailed him out, and he stayed with her in Staten Island. This was probably not good for our younger stepsiblings, but the boys loved John. They enjoyed having him around because despite his addiction, he was funny and entertaining. Unfortunately, he meddled with their upbringing, and this caused tension between John and my stepfather. He squandered their money despite their efforts to help him live a better life. They bought him a jeep and encouraged him to get a job. He disappeared for days at a time. He would sneak into the house late at night, setting off the house alarm. He sold some of my mother's possessions. He lied continuously and fabricated stories to get out of trouble. He bought drugs with the borrowed money. Drug dealers harassed my mother and threatened to kill John. She feared for his life. He spent too much time roaming the streets, begging for drugs, and spending the nights at strangers' homes. He almost overdosed and was found unconscious in a friend's apartment in Brooklyn. The years of addiction affected John's mind, and he was not able to think clearly. He visited extended family and spent much time with them. He loved our cousins very much but could not connect with them anymore. Each one moved on with their lives, completed college, and started working in their careers. They loved John, and he received their affection; however, it never filled his void. My uncles embraced him and opened their homes to him, but John was not stable and could not invest in deep relationships with anyone. This was a common trait among addicts. They were unstable and unable to commit to anything or anyone. However, John was unique, and though his relationships were shallow and strained, he continued to maintain them in the most loving way. It confused my family because he appeared well at times when everyone knew he wasn't.

He visited me in Virginia frequently and was devoted to my two daughters. He never missed their birthdays in October since their births in 1995 and 1997. He enjoyed the parties I had for them. Mark and I started a new life in Virginia, got involved in St. Mark Coptic Church, and made good friends. John became acquainted with our new friends and enjoyed their company. Drugs did not inhibit his charming personality. I learned later he smoked marijuana with some people from our social circle, and I was furious. It ignited a fight between us because I did not want him to bring his mess into my so-called "perfect" life. I enjoyed when he and my family visited, but I was embarrassed my friends would learn of John's addiction. Whenever I confronted him about the issue, his lifeless eyes showed no remorse. He was incapable of being sensitive to my feelings, though he genuinely tried. The drugs fogged his mind yet surprisingly his perception was still keen. Moving away gave me an opportunity to have a fresh start from my past. I did not want John to mar my image. I was too guarded to let my friends know of my past family history or drama. I lived a pretentious life, and it worked well for me. John was astute enough to recognize my hollow attempts to falsely represent myself and constantly called me out on it. He knew I had internal struggles and masked them well. I was always in survival mode and never paused to dwell on my struggles because I chose not to. Only John saw through me because I was a skilled performer, but he was more proficient in analyzing people. He was far more discerning than I understood. It was odd John could see through me when he was heavily drugged. I avoided John's confrontations and redirected him to focus on his addiction. Drug addiction seemed more afflicting than living a pretentious life.

Chapter 10
The Monastery

ONE DAY JOHN CALLED ME, and I knew immediately he was in trouble. He was delirious, and I could not decipher his words. He struggled to express himself. He told me he needed to borrow ten thousand dollars. I dropped the telephone. He fabricated a story about the debt he incurred, and once it was paid off, he promised to live a drug-free life. I really wanted to believe him, but I knew he was lying. John was relentless and persistent. He would not get off the telephone until I gave him a glimpse of hope. I told him I would discuss with Mark and let him know. I kept my word and asked Mark, not expecting an affirmative answer. Mark was willing to wire him the money but told me to get more information from John. He wanted to make sure John was, in fact, paying off debt and not using it for drugs. John swore and was willing to sign an agreement. He never proposed such an idea before, so it seemed authentic. He made me promise to not discuss the matter with anyone other than Mark, not even my mother. That was a red flag, but his proposed idea of a signed agreement was still convincing. I wanted to believe John. Shortly after I hung up with him, my mother called me frantic. She warned me John would contact me to borrow money. I debated whether or not to tell her the truth, and after careful consideration, I kept John's secret. John was already in his midtwenties, and I was eager for him to turn his life around. I was not aware of his disappearances, thefts, and deceitfulness. I did not realize he was still involved in gangs and drug trafficking. He seemed sincere in his desire to change, and for the first time, I detected fear. My mother must have sensed hesitation in my conversation, so she called again and divulged more information.

She gave John an opportunity to move away temporarily until things settled down. She wanted John to go to a monastery in Egypt and be under the care of a monk who was a psychiatrist. He was a close friend of the family and was willing to counsel John. John did not want to be counseled, so he left my mother's home and stayed at a friend's house. My mother could not reach him, but she knew he would contact me because he was in financial trouble. She knew of John's financial trouble from a loan shark who sent someone to collect the money owed. He was an illegal lender who preyed on John's desperation for money. When John delayed in paying off the loan, he sent someone to our mother's house. My mother and stepfather were terrified. He was courteous and revealed his identity. My mother was willing to listen to this man. He told them John owed his boss ten thousand dollars. My mother was dumbfounded, but she had no response to this man. She was inquisitive and wanted more details. Surprisingly, he was forthcoming and did not withhold any information. He even provided my mother with his boss's address. My mother felt awful for jeopardizing her family's welfare, and she had no excuses for John's carelessness. My stepfather was angry but knew my mother was not at fault. He did his best to support my mother and love John through this difficult time. My mother was a fearless woman and visited the loan shark. The big boss was stunned to see her. His hardened heart softened a bit. He could not turn my mother away because he saw the desperation in her eyes. She paid him ten thousand dollars and begged for John's safety. He gave her his word no one would harm John. My mother confronted John about the loan shark. John's eyes widened, and he stood in front of my mother, speechless. He was flabbergasted when he learned she went to the loan shark. He looked at her and asked if she knew how much she had endangered herself

My mother's response implored John to realize that he was the one who had endangered her. Though John was using drugs most of the time, he still had enough clarity of mind to identify his erroneous actions. He was grateful my mother paid off his debt but never circled back with me. He still wanted the money. John was definitely lying to me. She begged me to not lend John money because she wanted him to go to Egypt. She needed John to leave for a few months. I called him back and informed him I was not going to give him money. I encouraged John to regard our mother's advice. He was furious. His angry words hurt me, but I was not shaken. I knew I made the best decision for John. He abruptly hung up as I tried to defend my decision. John was disenchanted, and I needed to let him go. His anger was peculiar, and it triggered doubts. When I circled back with my mother, she warned me John would buy drugs with the money. It appeared he was in dire circumstances. It was tough to turn John away, but I wanted him to overpower his weaknesses. I knew a drug rehab facility would better serve John's needs. However, John was required to admit himself. John was not ready to take such a bold step. I wondered if being in Egypt would help him overcome addiction. I respected the monastery and the credentials of the monk psychiatrist, but I did not think they could handle the magnitude of John's drug problem. Frankly, I did not think anyone could handle John. Sadly, I believed lies and discounted God's promises. God's Word was the clear, concise, and absolute truth. Throughout my childhood years, I witnessed miracles and was still in awe. But when I faced a tough trial, I failed to trust that God had the power to heal John. It was an innate battle, a spiritual struggle I did not understand until I faced my own issues. I was awestruck by the miracles but never encountered the miracle worker. I observed healings but did not meet the healer. I knew God but had not personally encountered

Him. I was religious but did not have a personal relationship with Christ. Religion was essential, and apart from it, I would never have learned about God. But a personal, intimate relationship with the Lord brought heaven to earth. In Him, I would have been filled with peace and not rattled over John's life. The despair I felt during this disruptive decade was not John's addiction. It was not trusting God to see John through it. I did not pursue God's comfort, but His unremitting grace never failed me. When doubts inflicted mayhem, the Holy Spirit dispersed them. There was a calling on John's life to do great things. I did not know when and how. It was not my business to behold the answers to such questions. But of course, I made it my business because I thought I cared more about John than God did. It was absurd but true! My faith was shaken, and it became harder to keep my eyes on Jesus because John became my storm. I kept my eyes on John. I needed God to act quickly, but obviously, He had His own timing. In my distorted view of God, I also felt God owed my family because he took my father. Obviously, God did not owe me anything. His ways, plans, and thoughts were higher and better than mine.

After John arrived in Egypt, I anxiously waited for updates. One night I sat in bed, formulating different scenarios, and all of the outcomes were scary. Before we slept, Mark prayed for John and assured me he would be safe in the monastery. After tossing and turning endlessly, I finally slept. I had a dream about John. I saw him walking in the monastery, and he looked different. He radiated peace and joy. He looked happy. I started to walk toward him, but I stopped because someone had his arms around John. At first glance I thought it was the patron saint of the monastery, but the closer I walked towards John, the more I saw it was Jesus Christ. I sat up in bed, and my sudden movement startled Mark. I told him about my dream. Mark and I did not interpret dreams, but I thought it meant that John had died. Mark felt God was assuring me He was with John, in His arms. The next day my mother told me that John was going through withdrawal and that the process was repugnant. The monk psychiatrist closely monitored John and provided medical and spiritual care. John was still angry at me, but I knew he was not well. Months went by, and John started to feel better. He attended liturgies and midnight praises. I was not surprised to hear how much the monks grew to love John. He was a talented deacon in the Coptic church. He was gifted in playing the cymbals. He also chanted the deacon responses beautifully. John was not permitted to receive telephone calls, so I wrote him a letter. I encouraged him and shared my dream about him. John spent six months at the monastery. The monks were despondent to see John leave, especially the work crew. There was a farewell procession from the monastery to the car with many tears.

Chapter 11
Underground Drug World

JOHN AND I FINALLY TALKED, and he appreciated my letter. He cried when he read about my dream. He claimed it was God's promise that Jesus was with him always. He kept my letter in his Bible and read it daily. John was really grateful Mark and I never gave him the money. He was planning to buy more drugs but for the last time. John was planning to end his life. He wanted to overdose and die. He was depressed and hopeless. He wanted to be with my father in heaven. John knew suicide was not the answer, but he was desperate. He was scared to end his life because he knew it was not God's will for him. The time of respite was healing for John. After he returned from his trip, he started dating a nice girl he knew from high school. She came on a family vacation with us. My blended family started to mesh better, which made our vacations enjoyable. John improved daily and made better choices. Family gatherings were more pleasant and John was far more engaging than before. If I could save time in a bottle, this would have been the time. I wanted to preserve our happy days and make them last forever. Soon the bright days were darkened. John could not assimilate back into society, and he craved drugs. As a result, he made terrible decisions and disrupted our lives again. He cherished his girlfriend but was not able to give her what she needed. She cared for him but had no tolerance for drug abuse. John was smooth and savvy, so he talked his way out of their fights. She forgave him until he stole her car. He was driving with a suspended driver's license, which exasperated the situation. He disappeared for a few days. His girlfriend reached out to my mother. My mother advised her to call the police and report the car stolen. John's girlfriend was hesitant because she told my mother John could get arrested. That was my mother's plan. It was tough love. John was safer in jail than on the streets doing drugs. Once again, I was disheartened and discouraged. How was John ever going to get better? Every setback lasted more than my family could bear.

John denied the truth, but his erratic behavior instigated suspicions. Thereafter, one mishap led to another. We learned John spent most of his days in an underground drug world. He was evasive about his new abode and drug friends. John was working with dangerous drug dealers. He returned home weekly to collect money and some of his belongings. He was strung out and disheveled. My mother tirelessly pleaded with him. She was depleted of energy but never gave up on him. She questioned him about the underground places, but he was secretive. He lied about his whereabouts. She threatened to call the police, but he told her it would get him killed. He refused to disclose the name of the city because he didn't want her to look for him. I could not understand why John would spend his days in such despicable places. It sounded gross, dark, and terrifying. How could John tolerate being in such an environment? He just spent six months in a monastery. Surely, God wanted a better life for John. I wondered if my dream was a hoax. Mark was stronger in his faith and assured me repeatedly that God's plan for John's life would prevail. John was arrested for the stolen car. The Middletown police became reacquainted with John. Even they were distressed over his worsened condition. They watched John decline over the years. The arresting officer knew John would deteriorate and land in jail. He released him and encouraged my mother to find a rehab facility for John. While she was researching, John was arrested again. Someone leaked information to the police about John hiding drugs in our Middletown home. We assumed it was a parent of John's friend, but the identity was not our concern at the time. The police searched the home and found drugs, bongs, and other illegal supplies. The same arresting officer urged my mother to take serious steps to help John. He knew John had potential and did not want to put him away. The officer understood John's deeper issues and believed John could be helped. He saw in John unique traits that set him apart from other addicts. John's compassion, selfless love, and passion for people were palpable. The officer and John had great conversations behind closed bars. He knew this was a cry for help. John was suffering, but the officer firmly believed the proper response would spare John's life. I can write this now after thirteen years because hindsight is perfect. This officer was one of John's guardian angels. This man had enough evidence and reason to arrest John. But this was one time when I could easily see God being with John. I wanted to point that out because I missed it the first time. It was easy to overlook.

John was horrified after our home was raided. He was primarily concerned with the drug dealers' losses. Everything belonged to them. However, the discovery forced them to run the other way, and they left John alone. He was not welcomed back into their mess. John felt abandoned by them, and he was lonely. They had become his world and consumed most of his time. He was left to himself, and he spent most of his days sleeping and eating. He wanted to stay with me in Virginia, but I was hesitant. I knew he had drug connections in Virginia. He stayed with my mother and became more acquainted with Joey and Christian. He embraced them and enjoyed every moment he spent with them. They reciprocated his love, and John became their hero. They overlooked his drug addiction and took comfort in his interest in them. He lavishly gave his time and his undivided attention to them, and they relished both. He also amused them with his sense of humor. Despite his foggy mind and helpless disposition, he somehow found the strength to have controversial conversations with my stepfather about any topic. He knew our stepfather was good to our family and worked hard to provide for everyone. I knew John appreciated that about him. My mother did not appreciate John's contentions but was secretly hoping it was the beginning of a new life for him. She thought it was a perfect distraction from his other life. Well, this could have been the turning point, but of course, John could not leave well enough alone.

He went out one night. It always started with one night out. This was one of John's darkest and stormiest nights. This would have been the night John ended it all. He contacted a drug dealer and bought heroin and cocaine. He used both within the same hour and mixed them with alcohol. John took my stepfather's Volvo without his knowledge and drove with a suspended driver's license. He was intoxicated and drugged up, so he thought he was flying an airplane. In doing so, he crashed into numerous parked cars, damaging them all. Soon thereafter, he was being chased by the police. His velocity coupled with his ineffectual mind caused a collision. Remarkably, John was not harmed, and he fled the scene. The police chased him through the streets of Brooklyn, and four officers finally tackled him and then arrested him. The heroin, cocaine, and alcohol had hijacked John's brain and corrupted his ability to cooperate with the police. My mother was numb when the police called her. She was not aware John had left the house and driven off with her husband's car. She had no words, but she had the mind to tell the police to keep John in jail. She did not know how to respond but assumed the Middletown Police could help John. She no longer could. She gave them the contact information of the officer in Middletown. The Brooklyn officer was definitely stumped by John's unlawful deed, but he was more confused by his unusual response. John was not concerned about himself. He was more distressed over the possibility of harming others. John could have killed innocent people. He was perplexed by John's genuine remorse over hurting others. John's unease piqued the arresting officer's interest in him. In light of the arresting officer's conversation with the Middletown Police, he knew John was different. Because he spent several nights in jail, they spoke often. It took John time to recover from this horrendous drug abuse. Even he was flustered by it. For the first time, fear engulfed John, and he confessed his anxiety to the officer. John spoke extensively of our father and his yearning for him. He was not indifferent. He was suffering such deep agony. Despite John's pain, he noticed the officer flinch, unsettled. One of John's most unique traits was the ability to look past his suffering to see someone else's. John looked deep into the officer's eyes and saw a boy bruised by abuse. John knew.

The strong man who sat before John had suffered cruelty at the hands of his own father. The officer gulped when John broached the sensitive topic. The man's darkest and deepest secret was exposed by an inmate, a heroin and cocaine addict. The officer knew there was more to John. John's compassion unleashed hoards of emotions, and the officer shared his story. His dark journey of abuse steered him into the drug world, where he had stayed for years. Out of desperation, he cried out for help and was redeemed from the pit of destruction. This man faced hopelessness but ultimately found hope in Christ. He frequented Brooklyn Tabernacle, a thriving church in the area. The church community was vital to his recovery. He encouraged John to visit it. Several years later Brooklyn Tabernacle became a big part of John's spiritual journey. It was one of the churches John esteemed highly. It was no coincidence the arresting officer and John met on that dreadful night. As I look back today, I am confident it was designed by God. This was the turning point for John. The officer inspired John to go to rehab and pursue healing. He spurred John to embrace his Christ-like trait and become the radical change the world craves. John's compassion would hear smothered whimpers, uncover deeply buried wounds, and point people to Jesus. The officer still had a duty to enforce the law, and John was scheduled to appear in court. My cousin John F. represented my brother. My mother and stepfather were there to support John. It was a complicated case. Though the police dropped the charges, John was heavily fined. John was spared but knew there was a purpose. He wanted to honor the pact he made with the officer—not to fulfill a promise but to seek Christ. He knew he was at the end of himself.

John informed me of his Brooklyn calamity, but I was too sick to react. John could hear the weakness in my voice, but I masked it. I did not want my family to know I was suffering a painful colitis flare-up and was hospitalized. They had enough to deal with. I wanted John to focus on himself. John told me he wanted to go to rehab but was hesitant. He was afraid of the unknown. But the crippling aspect was not being able to overcome addiction. He believed the lies people invoked on him. I heard the desperation in his voice and implored him to seek help. I reminded him of my father's words that he would one day do God's work. He was a follower of God, but his fear and shame would prevent him from fulfilling his purpose. Just like God is building His kingdom, Satan is also expanding his. He cunningly uses people's failures to reject God. He wants people like John to be silenced and not live a fruitful life. I told John to fight back and resist the evil temptation. I promised he would overcome with Christ. John was encouraged but was still disturbed by my weak voice. He would not let it go, so I told him I was ill. I came home from work one day and could barely move. A friend from church encouraged me to attend Bible study. It was Wednesday evening. Danielle and Caitlyn completed their homework, so we could go to church. They begged until I forced myself out of bed. While driving, I became lightheaded, and the pain was unbearable. I knew it was serious, but I pushed through. I finally pulled over on the shoulder and dialed 911. I passed out before I could utter a word. I vaguely remembered Danielle jumping in the front seat. "There is something wrong with my mommy, and she needs help." I was conscious when the emergency team arrived. They felt comfortable with my health condition and drove Danielle and Caitlyn home before transporting me to the hospital. They asked my neighbor to watch the kids. I was then rushed to the hospital. Mark met me at the emergency room. My condition worsened and it appeared I was almost septic. Had I not attempted to go to Bible study, I probably would not have survived. John was discombobulated by my health deterioration. "Caroline, I am scared to lose you. You think God is punishing me? Am I stressing you out? Am I doing this to you?" I was exhausted, but I assured John ulcerative colitis was a complex autoimmune disease. John was disconsolate but I pleaded with him to move forward and not worry about me.

He went to the rehab the Brooklyn officer recommended, but he hated it. Upon entering it, he knew it was not a good fit for him. My mother withstood John's resistance and enrolled him in the program. After a few weeks of continued pleadings, my mother visited John to better assess his situation. When she visited, she understood why John was dissatisfied. One of the counselors recommended a men's rehab, America's Keswick in Whiting, New Jersey. He told my mother it was a Christian center, and it would better serve John. John wanted a time of respite at home before rehab, but my mother denied his request. Much to his disappointment, she drove him straight to America's Keswick. The ride between the two rehabs was long and unbearable for my mother because John was acting like an overgrown child. He was whining, complaining, and argumentative. She ignored his pleas and instead intrigued him with family updates. He called and told me about his experience at the previous rehab. I was a bit discouraged and hoped the next one would be better. We changed topics, and he wanted to hear about Danielle and Caitlyn. He was always interested in their lives.

Chapter 12
America's Keswick

DESPITE HIS STRUGGLES, JOHN WAS a wonderful uncle to my daughters. He enjoyed conversing with them and appreciated their advanced communication and social skills. He looked forward to being with the girls because they had outgoing personalities and cheerful dispositions. He valued their intellect and witty sense of humor. The rest of conversation was easy and pleasant. He and my mother turned into the long driveway into America's Keswick, and he let out a long sigh. His voice trembled. He was afraid of the unknown. We stayed on the phone for a few more minutes, and I encouraged him to have an open mind. Before we hung up, he said the property was serene and beautiful. He began to relax a bit as he detected a major contrast between the two properties. He told me to pray for him, and I prayed on the phone with him. I was nervous for him but was confident this was going to be a major turning point in his life. I had faith but still wondered why John had to go through this. My mother and John simultaneously felt the same level of peace as they drove on the property. Their nerves calmed, and the tension was released.

They were greeted by a man named John. He welcomed them with a cheerful smile and a hug for my brother. The greeting alone lifted my brother's spirits, and he relaxed. The representative explained the rehab program was solely a gospel-centered program.

My mother was hesitant because John already knew the Bible. She grappled with the gospel being the only source of treatment for John. He was a heroin and cocaine addict. She did not want to take John home, so she was left with no choice. She questioned the representative about medications to help John. The representative explained that addiction was not just a disease and that there were different approaches to helping an addict. He assured her the biblical program at America's Keswick was effective. She respected his solid faith and confidence in the program but was still skeptical. He diplomatically ignored her concerns and further explained John would also have chores. She was very much in favor of my brother laboring. The rehab was supported by a retreat center, and the addicts worked to keep the retreat area from being unkempt. They did laundry, vacuumed, cleaned, washed dishes, and cooked. John was tasked with laundry. He also told them John would attend a Bible study, group sessions, one-on-one counseling, and worship services and that he'd have personal quiet time to reflect on God's Word. They had a game room where men could play Ping-Pong, cards, and board games. They also set time aside for personal reading and could go to the library to check books out. John was most excited about the game room. But he was also thrilled about the library. Growing up, John enjoyed going to the library, and it wasn't because he was an avid reader. For some odd reason, he loved libraries, and he'd spent hours at our town library. He did not particularly like the rehab library and felt it was outdated. Otherwise, the ambiance of rehab was pleasant, and John's nerves settled down. He felt more relaxed, and the staff's friendliness eased his anxiety. There was a stark contrast between the previous rehab and America's Keswick. John was required to stay at least 120 days, and for the first thirty days, he was not permitted to receive visitors or telephone calls. Anxiety crept up on him again because he was in dire need of family support. John had no choice but to adhere to the rehab's rules. As my mother prepared to leave, John wept bitterly and wanted to go home.

Even though Keswick felt safe, John was still scared. My mother exercised tough love and walked away from John, knowing it would serve him well. It was refreshing but daunting.

She called me on her way home and bawled. She questioned her motivations and intentions. She knew she could no longer handle John, but she wondered if she was abandoning him. I reinforced her decision and told her she was not equipped to support him in the capacity he needed. She was not a trained counselor. John was in dire need of serious help, or he was going to overdose and die. The weeks that followed were tough because we had no contact with John. We were tempted to call America's Keswick but respected their rules. We were concerned over John's well-being and adjustment to the rehab. The long, drawn-out month was finally over, and my mother visited John for the first time. She cooked a feast and baked cookies for John. She made him his favorite food, chicken. John loved chicken and ate it every day. Everyone at America's Keswick was excited about our mother's visit because the aroma of the delicious food spread widely and quickly. The scent drew most of the men to the dining hall, so thankfully, she made enough food to feed an army. After everyone ate, our mother wanted to spend time with John. She perceived a change within him and was eager to hear about his experience. John was different. His demeanor was calm; he was bright-eyed and engaging. He introduced my mother to his new Egyptian friend, who became his best friend in the short month. John's affable personality was his redeeming quality, and people were easily drawn to him. John's friend already felt he was part of our family. He spent time with John and my mother. There were lots of tears and laughter. John's exuberant laughter triggered sweet memories for our mother. His old self was resurfacing. He finally spent time alone with our mother and shared his experience with her. My mother was in awe of the changes that had occurred within John. He was an extrovert yet valued his quiet time, meditating and studying the Bible. John, like me, never enjoyed quiet time. We preferred chaos. He breathlessly told our mother about the Bible studies, praise time, one-on-one counseling, and how much he learned of God's character and unconditional love. John yearned for God primarily because of our father's deep reverence and love for Him. Our father's relationship with God was inspirational but seemed too far-fetched for John. During his abbreviated time at Keswick, John's heart softened, and he sought the Lord for his spiritual enrichment.

There was also a supernatural transformation John could not elucidate to our mother. When he tried, words escaped him, and he just smiled. His smile spoke volumes. His change of heart was not complex, but such transformation was understood in the spiritual realm, not in the human mind. The brain could not fully encompass God and the way He touched people's hearts. Because John could not find his own words, he borrowed God's Word, which sprouted wisdom. John was keenly aware of the dramatic changes within him. His desire for God perplexed him too. John's heart was renewed, and he attributed it fully to the grace of God because it was not by his own power or doing. It did not make sense. His cravings for drugs and dependencies on them were vanishing. This was bizarre because he tried to stop many times and could not. John never wanted to become a drug addict, yet he chose daily for ten years to take drugs, never foreseeing the effect they would have on his brain. They temporarily erased the painful memory of his sufferings. John found being absent from his mind was painless because it made him think less of his loss. His feeble attempts to overcome addiction failed repeatedly because he overstimulated his system with drugs. Even when his body was depleted and became weak, his mind was in overdrive. Marijuana, heroin, and cocaine affected John's brain by disturbing its communication system. The chemicals flooded John's brain with dopamine, which made him feel great. At a normal level, dopamine was healthy, but the invasion of drugs increased its level, which had a euphoric effect on his brain and caused him to continuously crave drugs. His brain falsely communicated to his body that he needed drugs to be happy. However, John slowly discovered the years of smoking weed, cocaine, and heroin never filled his void because he was caught in a vicious cycle, and in the end, he still felt hopeless. The gospel approach at Keswick proved to be far more effective than my mother predicted. Just like drugs had the power to speak lies that John believed, the gospel had greater power to speak truth that John irreversibly received. He was healing because of the Word of God, the gospel of truth, and the power of God. The healing began, but it was an ongoing progression for years to come.

America's Keswick two-phase program was founded in 1897 by a dying alcoholic who was healed miraculously by the power of God. He built the rehab on the biblical principle that God was the only healer. The faith-based program did not utilize medical means to overcome addiction. Its most powerful weapon against the battle of addiction was the gospel of Christ. Withdrawal from drugs did not completely heal the addict, but it was the first step to liberation. As mentioned earlier, drugs interfered with the communication lines of the mind. John needed a sober mind in order to better understand the meaning of the gospel and its role in his life. America's Keswick did not prescribe medications to assist with the withdrawal process. They only accepted addicts who had gone through withdrawal. John had already gone through withdrawal in the previous rehab center, and it was rigorous. America's Keswick further expected the addict to enroll himself in the program and achieve a life-changing goal, namely spiritual transformation. Enrolling oneself did not benefit the rehab center but was of greater value to the addict. The addict had to be intentional about achieving his goal. Biblical truth gave John a new lens to see that the root of his struggle was a worship disorder. People will profusely argue this point, especially struggling addicts. This book was not intended to persuade my readers to accept this knowledge as their own but to merely share how this revelation changed my brother's direction. John learned he was created by God to worship God. Any other worship caused unrest for his soul. John deified our father, and when he suffered his loss, he replaced the void with drugs. His addiction was a sin because he replaced God with his desire for drugs, seeking false gratification. As he read through the four gospels in the Bible and reflected on our father's teachings, John started to view God differently. The God he experienced in the gospels was a loving, forgiving, nonjudgmental, and tenderhearted one. He was an awesome God. He was the God John desired to worship and have a relationship with. He liked God's approach, especially the way He interacted with the Samaritan woman in John 4. John was able to relate to her because he, too, felt ostracized and ashamed of his lifestyle. He adored the way Jesus spoke to her and personalized it. In his heart he heard Jesus tell him, "John, no matter what you did or will do, I love you very much. Follow Me and find rest in Me." And John did without hesitation. He wanted to be with that God for eternity and at any cost. He longed to be forgiven and loved. And the best news was that he was forgiven and loved because of the blood of Jesus.

In addition to the Bible, John enhanced his knowledge with a book that changed his whole perspective on addiction, *A Banquet in the Grave* by Edward T. Welch. In John's opinion, this was one of the best books on addictions. (If you are struggling with any kind of addiction, I strongly suggest you read this book.) The book is summarized as follows: "*A Worship Disorder:* Will we worship ourselves and our own desires, or will we worship the true God? Scripture reveals addicts' true condition: like guests at a banquet thrown by "the woman folly," they are already in the grave. Can we not escape our addictions?" Following Jesus, we have immense hope that God can give power so that we are no longer mastered by the addiction." Edward Welch affirmed the biblical teachings John was being taught. There was hope for addicts, and such hope was found in Jesus Christ. John wanted my mother to understand the impact of this book, but he could not eloquently describe it, so he read the reviews to my mother. John Freeman from Harvest described this book on the back cover. "One of the most helpful books providing practical theology on addictions. Welch's assessment of addictions as a problem that proceeds from the heart, involving issues of worship and idolatry, is central to helping people grow and change. This is vital reading for church leaders and for friends and family desiring to help those struggling with addictions." He read another raving review to her written by Peter Garich from the Dayspring Center for Biblical Counseling. "Destroys the myth that addiction is a disease and sin is a sickness. Welch shows that the hopeless cycle of 'sickness, recovery, and relapse' must be replaced with the biblical view of sin, salvation, and sanctification. As a pastor, biblical counselor, and redeemed (not recovering) ex-heroin addict, I believe Welch has given every pastor, parishioner, and anyone caught in the bondage of idolatry/addiction a biblical road map to freedom." And finally, the last review, which summed up Welch's powerful message, was written by Robert A. Emberger from the Whosoever Gospel Mission. "Biblically sound, practical, filled with Christ-like compassion … This much-needed book offers real hope and the promise of victory in Jesus to those struggling with addiction."

"Mom!" John exclaimed with great fervor. "All I needed was Jesus Christ!" John knew the journey ahead was not going to be easy, but he sought refuge in America's Keswick theme verse. "Therefore, if anyone is in Christ, he is a new creation. The old has passed away; behold, the new has come" (2 Corinthians 5:17).

Our mother was dumbfounded. Something was missing. The Bible rehabilitated John? He was already conversant with the Bible. John did not rationalize his reformation to our mother and accepted his transformation as a gift. Even if he tried to explain, he knew it was a God thing. It was the *mystic* power of God. John had no logical explanation. Therefore, he pointed my mother to the only answer, the Bible. In that short time span, John became well versed in the Bible. My mother was impressed with his increased knowledge but also overwhelmed with his peaceful demeanor. Even his mischievous smile was seasoned with joy, and his eyes gleamed with wisdom. John discovered happiness in the mundane chore of doing laundry. In addition to his assigned task, he helped with dishes and cooking. John hated chores. Growing up, he purposely broke dishes so he wouldn't have to do them. As their visit was coming to an end, my mother groomed herself for John's usual plea to leave. Much to her surprise, John extended his stay beyond the required months because America's Keswick was the solace he necessitated. He was in the infant stages of his spiritual development and wanted to grow deeper in his faith. He was also not prepared to assimilate back into society. He understood his limitations and chose not to overstep his boundaries. John was not the same person my mother had dropped off. She left the rehab with questions teeming in her mind. Who was this John? My mother believed in miracles but only the ones she read in the Bible. Was this a miracle? Was this for real? Why didn't this happen at the monastery where John was surrounded by holiness? It was happening in a place where men were broken, unstable, depressed, and hopeless. It did not make sense. It was unfathomable because we put God in a box and expected Him to work in a different way. We limited His celestial power and presumed He only used righteous people to transform lives. We never expected recovering addicts to point John to Jesus; we assumed it would be a monk who devoted his life to worshipping God. God used broken and despondent people just the same if not more. We were narrow-minded and expected God to adhere to a religious blueprint. Instead God's grace was sufficient for all sinners, and He worked through people who humbly submitted to Him. His strength overcame their weaknesses so that they could do His divine work. God did not commission qualified and righteous people. He prepared them through their sufferings. He communicated in different ways, and His manifestation is unique to each person. Saul's conversion in the book of Acts was one of John's favorite. Saul zealously persecuted Christians. Zeal was a desirable attribute when channeled properly. After his encounter with Christ, Saul became Paul and passionately changed the world with the New Testament. When God called people, He not only converted them but changed their names (Abram to Abraham and Jacob to Israel). At Keswick, John was among sinners who were redeemed and converted in order to heal addicts like him. The Holy Spirit changed their names too. In Christ, people assumed a new identity. They were called addicts by Satan, but God called them His children. John was among God's people.

It seemed futile that the Word of God had reformed John. I am ashamed to write such words, but I am being brutally honest. John heard the gospel throughout his life. He knew right from wrong and recurrently chose the erroneous path. Though I never forgot our father's words that John would one day do something magnificent for God, the ten dreadful years faded the memory. I started to think it was nearly impossible for John to be redeemed. John was staggered by my riposte. Our father assured John I would never give up on him. He recognized an obstinate spirit within me and knew my tenacious pursuit of people would prevail. Our father noticed my unique trait because I inherited it from him. Our father never gave up on people, and he saw the same fervor in me. I confess that was a power beyond my comprehension. I did not understand its value until later in life. I never gave up on John but foolishly thought God did. John reminded me of my humanity, which paled in comparison to God's divinity. My brother appreciated my ongoing support and relied heavily on me but realized I could not save him. No one could. He only had one Savior. I was enthused by John's spiritual reformation and clung to each word he spoke. The words resonated in my mind but took years to seep into my heart. John continued to share exultantly about his renewed mind. During his Bible studies at Keswick, John learned more about God's love than condemnation and judgment. He was released from the bondage of addiction and no longer felt entrapped. He repeatedly heard people call him a loser, so he believed it and lived it. When he heard God loved him unconditionally, he initially resisted accepting such foolishness. Why would God love an addict, a failure, a sinner? Why would God love someone who blatantly disobeyed Him? Why would God love someone who was destructive? God answered John. "But God shows his love for us in that while we were still sinners, Christ died for us" (Romans 5:8).

God was not waiting for John to change. He loved him first. In addition to his Bible studies at Keswick, our father's words resurfaced in John's heart. The same words echoed in John's mind even while he was in the underground drug world. But his heart was hardened, and he rejected them. During John's quiet times at rehab, God revealed to John that He was with him in that deep pit, fighting for him. John resisted Him. His body and spirit were at war because he knew the truth but believed the lies. He heard my father's words. He clearly heard God's voice but contravened them. He chose to nurture the evil within him and smite the good. John defiantly repelled God. Yet God pursued him staunchly. John felt God's deep love for him. His heart softened and received His love lavishly. The change in John's heart was radical, but his struggle did not change immediately. Jesus did not change John's situation. Instead he called John to follow Him. When the Lord called the disciples to follow Him, they took nothing with them. Following Jesus meant John had to leave everything behind and trust Him. Not many people could understand the enormity of such a calling. John did. He was willing to follow God's calling at any cost. God's will for John was to encompass hope, knowing his tribulation was part of the Lord's intricate design. John walked away from everything and followed Jesus. The road ahead was not easy. John knew he was going to walk through "the valley of the shadow of death" (Psalm 23:4), but he was no longer crippled with fear. Where there was a shadow, there was light, and he was no longer walking in darkness alone. He had the best companion. John was *walking through*, not *staying there*, and this insight filled him with hope. John was grateful for his suffering. "Count it all joy, my brothers, when you meet trials of various kinds, for you know that the testing of your faith produces steadfastness. And let steadfastness have its full effect, that you may be perfect and complete, lacking in nothing" (James 1:2–4).

John's gratitude cultivated a heart for Jesus. He aimed for heaven and shifted into a kingdom focused mind-set. He was thankful for his circumstances because they pointed him to Jesus. His grateful heart and joyful spirit in the midst of his crisis produced steadfast faith. John lacked nothing because he found it all in Christ alone. John reflected and learned valuable lessons from his fight with addiction. He imprudently resorted to his own resources and quickly learned they were purposeless. Apart from God, John was hollow. But he quickly learned that our father's time and words were never wasted. Our father had pointed John to the Only One who could salvage and redeem him. When John hit rock bottom, the Gospel became his rock. It came to life within John's heart and possessed an unrelenting power. There was divine power in God's Word, and it was no longer a compilation of bedtime stories. It became John's redemptive story. In the complete silence of his quiet times, he heard the Lord tell him that He would use his journey with addiction for His glory. John endured this trial so that he could be refined and purposed for an even bigger plan. John did not foresee the future but surrendered and trusted the omnipotent God he encountered daily. The meditation time became John's favorite part of his daily routine. He sat silently and soaked up the peaceful moment with Jesus.

My mother continued to visit John, and each time he grew stronger in his faith. He extended his stay despite the rehab's rules. His charming personality persuaded them to bend the rules. The representatives at rehab joked that John was above the law. His sense of humor was appreciated there, and they praised his contagious laughter. His spiritual growth impacted everyone at rehab and left a lasting impression on them. They did not want John to leave, but he had overextended his stay. It was time to say goodbye, and his farewells took a very long time. It was a Hanna trait. John was a bit frightened to step back into life, and he was not sure how he would assimilate into society. He knew he was not alone. He had the Spirit of God within him. John fought his fear with God's Word. It became his lethal weapon against Satan's attacks. The following words empowered John as he drove away from America's Keswick: "So do not fear, for I am with you; do not be dismayed, for I am your God. I will strengthen you and help you; I will uphold you with my righteous right hand" (Isaiah 41:10).

Chapter 13
The Renewed John

M Y MOTHER DROVE JOHN TO Staten Island to stay with her until his next step. He was received well by her husband and his sons. John loved Joey and Christian and was looking forward to being with them. His relationship with our stepfather was still a bit strained, but it was cordial. He could not wait to tell them about his rehab experience. At Keswick, he learned to never be ashamed of his journey but to embrace it as a life lesson. His conversations were lighthearted and engaging. He was excited to tell them about his new Egyptian friend, who later became part of our family. John was very helpful around the house, washed dishes, took the garbage out, and even cooked dinner. He made his bed daily and cleaned the house as needed. He started each day by meditating on God's Word. His company was pleasant, and he brought laughter into the home. As the months passed, John needed to move on with his life. He moved out, got a job, and applied to schools in the New York area. Despite these giant steps toward a better life, John slightly struggled. He was tempted daily with drugs, and each day he needed to make wise choices.

The harried life rattled John, and he was not able to focus on his goals. There were a few minor setbacks, but he was determined to persevere. His faith was barely shaken because He believed God would fulfill His promise. Despite his strong faith, he doubted at times. He spent time with family and close friends. They supported him spiritually and encouraged him to remain strong in his faith. They prayed for him, read the Bible with him, and invited him to church. John was accepted into college and worked diligently to graduate in three years. Secretly, he dabbled with drugs but not like the previous years. As a follower of Christ, he was not exempt from sin or temptations. At the beginning of his spiritual transformation, John thought his battle was over and would never touch drugs again. He quickly learned it was a journey. John mistakenly thought he would encounter God once and be forever changed. It was an ongoing encounter. He surmounted high hurdles but continued to face bigger ones. There were days he felt he was dying but knew God was not burying him. He was planting him. He needed to grow where he was being planted and not thwart God's plan. Such knowledge was powerful, and it stimulated John to fight with all his being. He pursued his degree vehemently, and while doing so, he became heavily involved with philanthropy work. He left no time for idleness because it exposed him to much trouble. He knew he could easily slip back into his previous vicious cycle. He acknowledged his feebleness and how it was debilitating. John was getting discouraged and was hesitant to confide in anyone. Family and close friends were overjoyed with his renewed life, and he did not want to disappoint them. Once discouragement crept into John's heart, he slowly recoiled, but it was subtle. The elusive change was not detectable, so it went unnoticed. It flustered John, but he resisted the urge daily to surrender to his weakness.

John finally confided in our cousin John F. He was like a brother to him, and he trusted him. My brother felt sad and guilty that he had been in rehab during our cousin's wedding. He always dreamed of standing beside him as a proud younger brother. John was granted permission to leave rehab just for the wedding day. As a result, he was not part of the wedding party. This was one of the many occasions my brother missed out on. He was grateful to have attended the wedding but was sad he wasn't fully present. His mind was distant, and he was disillusioned. Our cousin loved John unconditionally and never held it against him. If anything, John F.'s love for my brother only grew deeper. Knowing how much he was loved, my brother confided in him about his struggles. Our cousin was able to provide ongoing support and prayers. We were fortunate to be part of a family who believed in the power of prayer. Their faith was unwavering regardless of the circumstances. Most of the family slowly became aware of John's struggle and prayed for him.

John realized he relied more on himself and less on God's power. The conversion that began within John was real, and he tried to regain control and steer his life. When he was at his lowest point and had nowhere to go, he had no choice but to surrender. He was vulnerable and needed to depend on someone. Suffering causes people to cry out for mercy and help. Whether people believe in Christ or not, they cry out for help. They may not know who they are praying to but their anguish leads them to desperation. Despondency and misery brought John to his knees, and when he felt better, he regained his strength. When he reclaimed his ferocity, he fought for control over his spiritual transformation. John was slowly realizing he did not have divine power to do the work only God could do.

Chapter 14
Finally Got It

ONE NIGHT JOHN SUCCUMBED TO his nostalgias for drugs. His deep sorrow drenched his pillow with tears. Words from along ago haunted John, and he kept hearing them, "Once you're an addict, you will always be an addict." He was counseled at America's Keswick to drown out bad thoughts with God's Word. It was the eve of Thanksgiving Day, and John was alone. He remembered the wise advice and jumped out of bed to find his Bible. He read from Romans.

> For I do not understand my own actions. For I do not do what I want, but I do the very thing I hate. Now if I do what I do not want, I agree with the law, that it is good. So now it is no longer I who do it, but sin that dwells within me. For I know that nothing good dwells in me, that is, in my flesh. For I have the desire to do what is right, but not the ability to carry it out. For I do not do the good I want, but the evil I do not want is what I keep on doing. Now if I do what I do not want, it is no longer I who do it, but sin that dwells within me. (Romans 7:15–20)

John sobbed because he was enslaved by his sin. He wanted to stop taking drugs, but he continued to struggle. He reread the passage over again, but his eyes kept wandering to the plastic bag of cocaine on his nightstand. He understood the meaning of those profound words, but his body craved cocaine. He had not snorted cocaine since he had left America's Keswick. He occasionally smoked weed but not heroin and cocaine. He was excelling academically. He was adapting socially. He was reading scripture daily. But he wanted drugs. John began to question God's plan. Doubt crept into his mind and held him captive. He struggled to believe God could heal him completely from addiction. He was losing hope, but scripture was pouring into his mind like rapid fire. The battle intensified, and John was sweating profusely. He carefully set the Bible aside and walked slowly to the nightstand. But his knees grew weak, and John fell to the ground. He cried out to God for help. His addiction was stubborn and relentless, and it pursued John with force. His body shook, and his hands kept reaching for the plastic bag. The following words from Romans braced John: "But where sin increased, grace abounded all the more" (Romans 5:20).

John was overwhelmed with his sin. After reading Edward Welch's book on addiction, he learned addiction was not a disease but a sin. It was a sin because it kept him from God. However, God's grace was more stubborn and persistent. God's sufficient grace not only began the conversion process in John but pursued him as well. His sin increased as every second passed, but where was God's grace? Where was the increase? He believed God's Word had power, but John wasn't feeling the power because he was growing weak. He cried out to God, "My sins have overtaken me, and I cannot see. Come quickly, Lord, to help me" (Psalm 40:12–13).

Silence consumed the small bedroom, and John waited desperately on God. He refused to give up. He felt nothing and wept. He could not utter more words, and his heart ached terribly. His spirit groaned. He lifted up wordless prayers, and his tears became his prayers. He felt he had given it his all. He did all the right things to be in good standing with God. What more could he do? How much more would he need to sacrifice? The minutes were long, and hours were passing by. But John was still. He knew family and friends were gathering in preparation for one of his favorite holidays, Thanksgiving Day, but his heart and mind desired God. Nothing in the world at that moment mattered more. John could not even explain where the longing came from, but he knew it was far beyond his own understanding. Scripture ministered to John, and words poured into his heart. "My hope is in you. Save me from all my sins. I was silent; I would not open my mouth, for you are the one who has done this. Hear my prayer, Lord, listen to my cry for help; do not be deaf to my weeping" (Psalm 39:7–9, 12).

As John continued to be still, God's plan unfolded, and it became clear that his addiction was part of the preparation for his next season in life. Though John knew this and was filled with unexplainable peace, he questioned his tumultuous journey. The amalgamation of peace and turbulence at that very moment baffled John. He could not make sense of what was happening to him, and he felt he was having an out-of-body experience. His mind kept wandering to the darkest moments of his addiction, and the images were gruesome. His mind became a battlefield, and God's Word became his weapon against the dark forces. He was filled with the Holy Spirit, and the supernatural power steered his mind so that he recalled the childhood Bible stories our father told us. He immediately thought of the story of Joseph in the Bible. As a young boy, he enjoyed hearing that story because in the end, Joseph was a hero. Joseph first endured tough times like being sold as a slave by his brothers. Then he was imprisoned wrongfully. No one escaped evil, not even a good man like Joseph. But God brought good out of evil, and Joseph became a leader. His brothers were at his mercy, and he opted to honor God by not seeking revenge. Instead he showed love to his brothers because he was filled with the spirit of God. But it took time.

Joseph was chosen by God, and even as he suffered dark days in prison and was alone, God was with him. In the end, God esteemed him highly and honored him. God used his difficult circumstances for good. Joseph was not the only Bible character John thought of. The Bible was comprised of good coming out of evil and God bringing beauty out of ashes. In light of his insurmountable obstacles, John was soon filled with hope. He felt something different, and his limited understanding of God expanded. John came to the end of himself. He was depleted of energy, and his strength failed him. But God was not failing him. John misconstrued God and His plan. What he failed to understand was that God's plan was infallible and that it was designed specifically for him, even the addiction. Don't get me wrong. God did not want John to be an addict. That was John's choice. God does not cause us to sin. We are enticed by our own desires. John's addiction was no surprise to God, but He did not choose it for John. God did not abandon John as he drowned his sorrows in drugs. He showed up every time to remind John he was loved unconditionally despite his mistakes. But there were consequences to his decisions. He was not being punished because the ultimate punishment happened on the cross when Jesus died for his sins. Discipline was and continues to be part of God's plan for His children. Parents understand this concept well. John waited patiently because he felt something was stirring within him, and it was different than any other experience he encountered. He was consumed with mixed emotions. John contemplated ending his life because he could not bear the sufferings any longer. The internal agony was intense, and he was in great despair. He remembered when the righteous prophet Elijah wanted God to end his life too. But God said no because He was ready to use the prophet to change the world. Every encounter with God impacted the world. God commissioned John too, but he feared addiction because it was a losing battle. Despair and discouragement accompanied John as he tried to grasp truth and freedom. He was feeble, but as he emptied himself completely, confronted his addiction, and labeled it as sin, John began to feel relief and comfort. A huge burden began to lift from him. He knew addiction was a disease, a sickness, but he also recognized his sinful desire in pursuing it fiercely. Once again, I want to be sensitive to other addicts and not focus on addiction being a sin.

But this was John's story, and it was how he viewed his addiction. It is also noteworthy to explain sin is a separation from God. John's addiction separated him from God, but it did not stop God from pursuing him. John reflected more on God's holiness and less on his addiction. God's beauty overcame the ugliness of addiction, and it no longer had a tight grip on John. His fear was dispelled. His weakness was overcome with God's strength. John was being renewed, and he prostrated before God in awe of His glory. John's inglorious past was no longer in sight. It was overpowered with this glorious experience. When he later described this moment to me, words escaped him. It was a personal encounter between God and John in the spiritual realm. I don't have words to accurately describe that special moment, so I will leave it alone. Anyone who experiences God at that level understands its depth and beauty.

John got it. It took years of suffering and agony, but John finally got it. Those were the words he excitedly told our cousin. His exact words were, "John, I finally got it!" He understood he must decrease so that God could increase and reign in Him. John surrendered completely and never looked back. He stumbled and struggled but stayed on the course and fought the good fight. The words from Psalm 103 ministered to him. "Bless the LORD, O my soul, and forget not all his benefits, who forgives all your iniquity, who heals all your diseases, who redeems your life from the pit, who crowns you with steadfast love and mercy" (Psalm 103:2–4).

John was in the pit and could not find his way out. He thought the only escape was to end his life. God fulfilled His promise and redeemed him. God showed up. Not only was John's life redeemed, but he was esteemed highly by God. The Lord's favor was upon

John, and He sanctioned him with the ineffable strength to do implausible work. John successfully completed college, graduated with honors, and got a job with a church in Nyack. He was an associate pastor and ministered to drug addicts in prison. John reached these young men with the gospel that saved him. His ministry was effective and life-changing because he was once one of them. Addicts listened to John. His charming and engaging personality immediately captivated them. His sense of humor and laughter eased tense moments and addicts held onto every word he spoke. When I first learned to play golf, my husband told me to let the club do the work because it was designed to hit the golf ball with force. In the same manner, John believed the gospel did its own colossal work, and he was just an instrument in God's hand.

People were not prepared for John's transformation because it was unfathomable. They did not know how to process John's conversion and wondered if it was authentic. On the other hand, some friends lost contact with John and thought he was still an addict. He never defended himself. Even when people continued to label him an addict, he did not correct them. He laughed it off. It actually irked me when he did that, especially when he ran into an old friend in Nyack at a gas station. This person constantly demeaned John. I hated the way he judged and ridiculed my brother. But people's judgments no longer bothered John. He was focused on his ministry. It became his sole purpose in life, his primary mission. He was determined to help people who were hurting, so he first reached out to the Coptic church because he knew Egyptians would never speak up. It was cultural to mask the truth to preserve the family's dignity. The priest John approached did not think the church was ready to deal with such issues yet. He was also concerned about John's past struggle with drugs and the negative impact it would have on the church youth. John respected his decision.

One of John's most admirable qualities was his humility. He was meek and emptied himself of superiority. Instead of growing resentful or feeling rejected, John did not react to the priest but responded to God. This was a refreshing retort, and it cleansed John's heart to hear God's voice. John was moved to be a voice for the mute, eyes for the blind, and feet for the lame. His heart ached terribly for people who were hurting, and he always said, "Hurt people hurt people," which caused sufferings to spread widely. It was an endless cycle, and people got lost in it. John wanted to give them aspiration by sharing his journey with them. He wanted people to understand that suffering was painful but there was hope. When he was in the underground drug world, the deepest fit he fell into, John felt God's presence. "God ... shouts in our pain" from C. S. Lewis's book *The Problem of Pain* was one of his favorite quotes. John's spiritual strength vested him to serve in other capacities. He was confident God had a different direction for his ministry. He prayed for guidance with patience. His faith continued to grow, and he never lost heart.

John enjoyed his associate pastoral work at the church in Nyack. He continued to visit addicts in prison, and he presented their cases in court. He was able to work with a judge in Nyack and plead the addicts' cases. The judge released juvenile addicts to John, and he would drive four hours each way to enroll them into Keswick's rehab program. The judge was amazed by the changes that happened in these young addicts' lives. The judge was of Jewish descent but did not deny the role of the gospel of Christ. He was actually intrigued by it because he witnessed lives being rehabilitated. When addicts reappeared in court, he immediately documented their changed demeanors and aspirations to overcome addiction. Though he did not grasp the work of the Holy Spirit, he was keen enough to recognize a supernatural transformation that went beyond human power. In most cases, these young people were already employed when they reappeared in court, which facilitated the judge's decision in releasing them. John wanted to ensure they would assimilate into society, so he helped them find jobs and housing. John and the judge formed a strong bond built on mutual trust and respect.

Any person who encountered John even once was immediately part of his friend circle. He could make you feel you were his best friend. This judge was no exception, even though they came from different walks of life. I was very grateful for this man who believed in John's work regardless of his past mistakes. He never judged John for his past but instead respected his prudence because of it. This was refreshing for John, and it was the beginning of God's promise unfolding in his life. The judge continued to work with John, and many juveniles acquired a second chance in life. Because John spent many hours in the car, he would call me daily at ten o'clock in the morning. He invited me to pray for the young addicts, and I learned each one had a story. Like John, I was always interested in people's stories and backgrounds. I loved hearing them from John's perspective because it was verbalized with mercy and compassion. What I appreciated most about John was he never labeled an individual based on religion, race, or anything other than being a child of God. Whenever he shared someone's story with me, he told me that they were broken but that there was hope. John never felt that anyone was broken beyond repair, and he also believed love healed all wounds. So John loved with all his heart. It embodied God's love. "Love is patient and kind; love does not envy or boast; it is not arrogant or rude. It does not insist on its own way; it is not irritable or resentful; it does not rejoice at wrongdoing, but rejoices with the truth. Love bears all things, believes all things, hopes all things, and endures all things. Love never ends" (1 Corinthians 13:4–8).

I have read that passage many times, and the last few words perfectly described John's love. John never stopped loving a person. He never gave up on people. He possessed the same trait our father did. Just as John was relentless in so many ways, his love was relentless.

Chapter 15
John's Conversations

A FEW OF OUR LAST CONVERSATIONS never made sense until 2005. It was October 2004, and John drove down for my daughters' birthday party. After the party we were standing in the master bedroom, and I had a picture hanging on my wall because it always reminded me of my father. It was called "The Faithful Servant." It was an image of Jesus Christ standing in heaven, embracing a man, and the picture reads, "Well done, good and faithful servant. Enter into the kingdom of Heaven." John wanted to know what the picture meant to me. His question was purposeful. My response was direct and simple. "This was Daddy's entrance into heaven." John chewed on my response and nodded pensively. He shared his reflection on the picture. He calmly told me he longs to be that young man in the arms of Jesus. I looked at him with sadness and asked why he wanted to die. But he told me there was no death in Christ. He looks forward to being with God for eternity. "For the longest time, I wanted to die to escape the harshness of this life. For years I wanted to flight addiction. And of course, I just wanted to be with Daddy. But now I just want to be with my Lord for eternity and rest in His kingdom." I told him I did not want him to die. We promised to do life together. He looked at me and repeated, "There is no death in Christ. We will never die. We will be promoted from this life to the best life." He smiled and walked away. I pondered our conversation for days and kept mulling over the fact John was different, but I did not fully get it.

We had another conversation that also did not make sense until 2005. John was dating a beautiful girl who he loved and cherished. I was grateful for how much she reciprocated his love. John was unique, and it took a special woman to meet him where he was. One day he called to tell me he was planning to propose to her and could not wait to marry her. I was excited because I wanted him to get married and be happy. We hung up the phone, and I daydreamed about our future lives raising our kids, traveling and spending the holidays together. After a few minutes, he called back and sounded troubled. He was scrambling for words but finally collected himself and told me he was going to share something intimate. He warned me it was going to sound bizarre. He proceeded to say, "Caroline, I don't understand what I am about to tell you, so please listen. I still want to get married, and I already have Mom's wedding ring that Daddy gave her. I will propose, but I don't think I will ever actually get married." I did not understand what John was trying to explain to me. He simplified it and basically said, "I don't think it is God's plan for me to be married. I think He has a different plan for my life." I did not know how to respond. He realized it sounded absurd, so he dismissed his strange feeling. He ended the conversation by telling me he needed to confide that in me. The conversations continued and each one left me baffled but not completely perplexed. I knew John's relationship with God was intimate. I did not understand the depth until much later in life.

John called me the next day to tell me about his dream to build a library at Keswick Rehab. I thought it was a great idea, but he needed ten thousand dollars. He was recruiting me to help him with this prolific project. The library was one of John's favorite places at Keswick, but it needed to be updated. I admired John's desire to give back to the community that invested in him. He was thinking of the young men at the rehab and the value of having a quiet place to study, work, and read. I encouraged him to put this idea on the back burner until another time. With humor and lightheartedness, he asked if we could also put the halfway house plan on the back burner too. It was another idea that required money we both didn't have. He wanted to build a halfway house because he understood the complexity of addicts assimilating back into society. He attempted to convert our family home. The county denied his request because we lived in a residential community. John was a visionary and never gave up on his dreams. He had faith his ideas would come to fruition, even if he was not around to see them.

The holidays were John's favorite time of the year, but in 2004, Christmas was different. We could not locate John on Christmas Eve. We postponed dinner, but he never showed up. My maternal uncle, who adored John, was irritated and left disappointed. We were gathered at my mother's house in Staten Island. John finally showed up at eleven o'clock at night. Angry emotions were elevated, and John was the target of interminable questions about his whereabouts. John was exceptional at not reciprocating heightened emotions, so he calmly explained he was shopping for Christmas gifts. We were surprised because first of all, John never bought presents for anyone and second, he was empty-handed. Apparently, he was launching a new ministry at his church for the homeless. He bought hats, gloves, and scarves and assembled gift bags to distribute on Christmas morning. He rented a food truck for a few hours to provide warm breakfasts, coffee, and tea. He excitedly shared his plan with us, hoping we would join his church the next morning. He wanted to give hope to the people who needed it the most. We stared back at him with perplexed looks. We responded negatively. We did not want to wake up at the crack of dawn to stand in the blistering cold on Christmas morning with strangers. Selfishly, I wanted to be with my family in the comfort of our home on Christmas morning. I did not want John to go either. John did not make us feel guilty. Christian was the only one interested in accompanying John. John was his hero, and he would jump at any opportunity to spend time with him. We tried to coax John into canceling his plans but he refused. His heart was set on spreading the good news about the birth of Christ.

The next morning John and Christian went to Penn Station in Newark, New Jersey, for a few hours. They could not wait to tell us about their new Christmas experience. John spoke exuberantly of the hope the homeless people felt that morning. They gathered around the food truck and filled their plates with eggs, pancakes, bacon, sausage, and bread. They drank coffee and tea, which warmed their frigid bodies. John and his church distributed Christmas gift bags filled with hats, scarves, and gloves. John's favorite part was when he shared the message of Christmas with them. They gripped every word John spoke about baby Jesus and the joy His birth brings to the world. Their faces lit up when John told them Jesus was born just for them. He came into this world to give them eternal life. He promised their homelessness was a temporary affliction and the new life was free from suffering. He lifted their lowly spirits when he told them Jesus wanted to dwell in their hearts. His indwelling brings peace, joy, and love. He implored them to open their hearts and accept Christ as their living Savior. These people were stripped of everything. It may have been their own doing or the harshness of life, but regardless, they needed the love of Jesus. John gave them the best Christmas gift, and it was wrapped in the message of the gospel. They joyfully sang Christmas carols for hours and celebrated their first unsurpassed Christmas.

We begrudgingly listened to John and were selfishly focused on our Christmas morning. John sensed our apathy and was mindful of our indifference. He did not judge us but pointed us to the true meaning of Christmas. John never grew weary of doing good and honoring God. He was relentless. He suggested we read the Christmas story in the Bible. Mark did the same annually. They both agreed it was the right way to start Christmas morning. We opened our Bibles, and the ambiance improved. Heightened emotions settled down, and there was an aura of tranquility. John insisted my young daughters read the passages. Caitlyn was in the second grade, and Danielle was in the fourth grade. He appreciated their presence. John's best friend from the rehab spent the holidays with us. He was stupefied by John's spiritual transformation. He was a bit irritated with John's suggestion and was deeply concerned about John's radical change. He shared his concerns with me, and I laughed them off. I was baffled by John too. As the girls took turns to read, John gazed at them with admiration and respect. He appreciated how well they read. We concluded our Bible reading and briefly discussed the true meaning of Christmas. It was a better ending to the morning.

John pulled me aside afterward and shared his vision for Danielle and Caitlyn. He was confident both my daughters were going to be life-changers. John felt Caitlyn was most like him. He detected compassion and fervor within Caitlyn's heart. He claimed she would fight for the weak. I glanced over at Caitlyn. She looked so young, pure, and innocent. John knew his words stirred mixed emotions within me. For the first time, I shared with John my stance regarding Caitlyn. I only told a few people because it rattled me. John was struggling with drug addiction when Caitlyn was born in 1997. I never had the opportunity to tell him what happened the day Caitlyn was born. He listened intently as my eyes welled up with tears. When the doctor placed Caitlyn in my arms, I sensed in my heart Caitlyn was anointed by God to serve Him. The message was clear, but I thought my exhaustion engulfed my mind. Therefore, I rejected the thought. I was not ready to share Caitlyn. Admittedly, I was weak in faith and not ready to surrender to God's plans. When my mother and stepfather visited me, my stepfather shared the same feeling. It shook me a bit. Then the newly assigned priest from St. Mark's Church visited me in the hospital. Astoundingly, he had the same feeling when he held Caitlyn. My heart sank further, and I did not know how to respond. During her toddler years, Caitlyn was a prayer warrior. My friends coveted her prayers because they were sealed with a solid faith. As a child, she boldly proclaimed Jesus's love to the neighborhood kids. I respected her zealous spirit, but it was stained with anxiety. Therefore, John's words alarmed me, though I never dismissed what I felt in my heart for years.

John slightly disregarded my heightened emotions and redirected me to his vision. He wanted me to trust God's plan for my children. He knew I revered God but felt I idolized being a wife and mother. From his past experience, he understood the desire to implement plans not ordained by God. He saw the same struggle within me. He was concerned I would struggle to relinquish control. And I would be blinded by my agenda and overlook things. For instance, John repeatedly mentioned Danielle was suffering internally. She was stuck in a dark place and could not find her way out. He urged me to be attentive to her needs and stifled cries. He promised God would use her suffering for good. Danielle was only nine years old, and she had no life experience just yet. She was struggling but not to the extent John had mentioned. I was offended because he questioned my motherhood. I was too proud to allow my younger brother to counsel me about my daughter. My response did not hinder him. He further advised me to change the way I dealt with Danielle. He was not pleased with some of my dealings with her. He cherished Danielle and highly valued her leadership and interpersonal skills. He admired her joyful spirit and gregarious personality. He had the audacity to tell me I was blowing out her flame. I was thunderstruck. He placed his hands on my shoulder and told me he shared his heart with love. He cared about my family and wanted me to surrender them to God. I honestly had no idea what that meant. Since I was eight years old, I was in control and have not stopped since. I resolved every issue we faced. I never paused. Fear gripped me tightly as John's words struck me. I was not ready for a jarring journey. John detected my fear and planned to visit after Christmas to help me sort through my issues. I felt vulnerable and welcomed his planned visit.

John stood quietly to give me time to process. Normally, silence would create an awkward moment. Surprisingly, the quiet moment gave me an opportunity to gaze at John. He was different. John was a new man. He was not the same John whose countenance was tinged with pain. He was unshackled from despair and lived with hope. He used his brokenness to mend others. He no longer lived in shame. His circumstances humbled him and stripped him completely of himself. John became empty. He became nothing so God could fill him, and God became his everything. The few moments of silence were broken by his placid words.

"Caroline, today I experienced the true meaning of Christmas," he said. "Jesus Christ left His beautiful kingdom where He reigned in glory. There was no room for Him, so He was born in a stable among the animals. But He came to receive us with arms open wide on the cross. He reconciled us to His Father, to give us peace, love, joy and eternal life. You and I were privileged to grow up with this gift of knowledge, and we need to pay it forward. Christmas is celebrated by sharing the love of Jesus Christ with others. Today I understood the true meaning of Christmas. You will not find it in the wrapped gifts under the tree or in the comfort of your own home. It is stepping out in love and sacrificially giving to others. The world diluted Christmas and watered it down to materialism. People will always want more. But in Christ, you have it all. I look forward to making this my new tradition, and you are welcome to join me in bringing hope to the hopeless."

John was right, but I was overwhelmed. I was not ready to grasp and apply his words. He continued, "Caroline, your heart is deeply troubled. You single-handedly carried our family's burdens, and you are weighed down. I would not be the man I am today if it wasn't for your love and perseverance. Daddy was right. You never gave up. You were always there. I am not ignorant of the impact it had on you. And you continue to carry heavier burdens, but you need to release them. There is no grievance too big for God's forgiveness. I don't know what you are hiding but remove your mask. It disfigures your face and hides your true beauty. God did not make a mistake when He created you. He knit you together perfectly, and even your flaws are part of His grand plan. Your personality traits are unique to you, and they are fashioned perfectly by the Creator. You have a dynamic personality, and people are drawn to you. You are gifted in the way you touch people's hearts, but you are holding back. Let go and walk in freedom. Jesus forgives your sins, Caroline. You are beautiful, and I never met a person like you. I am honored to be your brother. I know you will do amazing things for God. He wants to use you, but you won't let Him. You live to please people, and you have become a prisoner in your mind. Your mind has become a battlefield, and you are trying to fight alone. And I don't blame you. You have been fighting for me for years since you were a little girl. But I am telling you today to please keep your eyes on Jesus Christ. The road ahead of you will be long and tiresome, but you are not alone. The Lord is with you and will permit trials and tribulations to refine you. Be prepared to receive God's plan and be willing to accept the good and bad. God will use the bad for good. He brings so much beauty out of ashes. I look into your eyes and see so much pain. Any struggle you are facing today is a result of a broken relationship with God. It's that simple yet so complex. You need to let God reign in your heart and guide you. His grace is sufficient for you. The Lord loves you so much, Caroline. He left ninety-nine sheep to come seek you, just you. Whatever you are hiding in the darkness, bring it to the light because Satan does his best work in darkness and isolation. No matter how afflicted you feel in life, you will never be crushed. Even when you are down, you cannot be destroyed because you have Jesus Christ within you. When you have Christ in you—and I mean really have all of Him in you—nothing in this world will ever tremble you, nothing!"

Tears trickled down my face, and John nodded with sympathy and compassion. I am never at a loss for words, but they escaped me at that moment. I maintained my composure because it was what I did best. No matter how I felt, I did not want people

The Beginning Starts at the End

to detect my weakness. My fortitude was my greatest obstacle, though I mistakenly thought my strength equipped me to face any challenge. John wanted his words to take root because he knew they echoed in my heart and mind and would make an impact one day. He embraced me warmly and held me longer than he ever did before. He looked forward to his visit in a few weeks, and so did I. He wanted to become better acquainted with the girls and spend quality time with me. He was hoping to visit Danielle in school and have lunch with her daily. John's requests were always ludicrous, but I told him I would check with her teacher. Then he thought he and I could spend time talking and meditating on the Bible. He wanted me to get a deeper understanding of God's grace and forgiveness. It sounded like a good plan, and I was looking forward to it. I let my guard down with John and was ready to share almost everything with him. I started to trust him. I knew he was genuine and would never judge me. I felt safe with him. We spent a wonderful Christmas Day with the family, filled with lots of food and laughter. John insisted we visit our father's family in Ridgewood, New Jersey. We stopped spending Christmas with them, but John insisted. For the first time, the entire family went.

We all piled up into our mother's GMC truck, and John drove. He made us laugh the whole ride there. We had a wonderful time with our extended family. On our ride back to Staten Island, everyone slept except John and me. John was driving and looked up at the rearview mirror. He told me this was the best Christmas since our father had passed away. I nodded in agreement. He looked up at me again and said, "Caroline, we are fortunate to have our uncles and aunts. They're not getting younger, so we should spend more time with Daddy's family. They love us so much. And you just never know who won't be around next Christmas. So let's spend as much time together." I smiled back at him and promised to make a better effort. When we arrived in Staten Island, everyone slept. John and I were still awake. He told me he needed my help with our mother and Jackie. He said that

Jackie thought he was too religious and that Mom was too proud to heed his advice. He was convinced I would be more effective in reaching out to them and guiding them to the Lord. He knew they loved God, but John's hope was for everyone to be filled with Jesus Christ. He even expressed concern about some of our friends in Virginia. We met them through my cousin, John. My brother really cared about them and wanted to share the love of Christ with them. I responded honestly and told John I didn't know how to preach Christ. He told me he would visit with them when he came to Virginia in January. And he reminded me it wasn't our job to convert or change people but to share the love of Christ with them.

After returning to Virginia, my heart softened a bit. I was too guarded to realize my heart was hardened. I agreed to spend New Year's Eve in church. Mark insisted we should spend the evening at church. He said it was the right way to start the New Year. I had no desire but agreed it was best for our family. In church I kept thinking about my conversations with John. I knelt down in church and prayed to God, seeking His help. I wanted to change. I promised God I would seek His kingdom and focus on my relationship with Him. I felt great about my new spiritual disposition. I shared my spiritual goals with John, and he was delighted to hear the excitement in my voice. He said when he came down in January, we would spend time in prayer. He wanted me to make peace with a friend. I referenced this issue in the foreword, and it was a situation that hurt me deeply. John encouraged me to humbly ask for forgiveness. I was taken aback because I was wronged too and deserved an apology. After a few more conversations with John, he helped me see the situation objectively. I recognized my role and better understood the need to ask for forgiveness. I wasn't ready because pride consumed me. John promised God would rid me of pride as I continued to pray. He reminded me only God changed hearts. I did not feel the change in my heart yet. Honestly, I neglected my situation, and it was easier to avoid my friend. John knew I was not a confrontational person, and it was not because I pursued peace. It was primarily due to the fact I did not want to confront my issues. I mastered the ability to move past my hurt. I tended to do that more often as I grew older. John recognized the pattern and was concerned about my inner struggles. New Year's Eve came to an end, and I was glad to see 2004 behind me. I was looking forward to 2005. I decided to follow Jesus and become more like John. I was aware my inner strength was a stumbling block but trusted John to lead the way. With great hesitation, I was letting go.

Let's pause here for a moment before reading the final part. If you are like me, then you will understand what I am about to share. I knelt in church before God and promised to follow Him. I was ready to surrender and be transformed into His likeness. As an infantile Christian, I expected life to be perfect and for all my past issues to dissipate immediately. Frankly, I looked forward to a comfortable journey. Well, my high expectations were not met as I desired.

John and Caroline – Last Christmas Together

John and Caroline – toddler years

John and Caroline with their father

Caroline, John and Jacqueline pictured at Public School 35

John's Parents, Aida and Kamal Hanna

Caroline's family - Caitlyn, Mark and Danielle Guirgis

John Kamal Hanna

Caroline, John and Jacqueline

Jacqueline's family – Michael, Alexandra and Helena

John wrote this letter one month before he passed away.

Dearest Mom,

I have been wanting to write this letter for the longest time but I couldn't do it. Thank God it's not too late. I want you to open your heart and mind very wide and read the following letter with complete understanding. I want to begin by asking you to excuse me for my lack of appreciation or shall I say lack of expressing myself for every wonderful thing you've ever done for me.

In case you didn't know, you are the world to me and you always will be. I know it's hard to believe but I strive to make you the happiest person on earth. We definitely have to solve our misunderstandings, lack of communication, and lack of trust which clearly stem from me. I am going to proceed with this letter with extreme sincerity, so sit back and relax.

I have always been a rebellious and stubborn person all my life. Growing up, I understand now you wanted me to be the best and maybe came down on me too hard. That was taken the wrong way by me and distanced me from you. I want you to understand I am a very emotional and sensitive person but lack expression. When I wasn't allowed to go out and play with my friends, I interpreted that as lack of love and terrible on your part. When you used to beat me with the belt, I used to go to my room, cry and say to myself 'she doesn't love me or care about me.' Now I realize I was sadly mistaken. Those actions and lessons you gave me in life were positively meaningful and very caring. Once again, you were raising me to be the best. I perceived all that very immaturely and with a narrow mind. I began avoiding you and turning to my father for sympathy, and he offered it in abundance. He was always there, like you, but I'll get into him later. Basically, I chose to run away from your heart but I always knew in my thick head that your heart was the warmest place in the world. Whenever I ran into a dead end, I always ran back to your heart temporarily, then run away again. Every time I ran away, I've gotten lost and I concluded I don't want to continue my life this way. I'm eager to crawl my way back into your heart and remain there.

As far as my father and you are concerned, I have to say I was very unreasonable. I never listened to your true feelings on the church matter.

The situation upset my father very much. I know one thing that he loved you to death, and it had to be for good reasons. I seemed to neglect that part and only see matters on the surface. He also may have lacked ambition and drive in life as you wanted. But I'm sure you wanted him to be very successful so we can lead a happy life as a family. He also may have lacked emotions and expressiveness, who knows? However, we have to let him rest in peace and proceed with our lives positively together. The fact that you remarried made me very mad also. Again you wanted us to have everything and you grasped every opportunity. I realize now that you tried everything in your power to show us the best life. I hold nothing against you once and for all.

This is not a letter of sympathy, but on the contrary. I'm not looking for sympathy but encouragement and most importantly your dearest blessings. Understand that this is not a letter from a lost person but a new person. I am looking forward to the next steps in life and I definitely need you and your blessings to become successful and happy.

Mommy, there isn't enough paper to thank you for everything in life. You've been nothing short of wonderful and I haven't realized it 'til now. I want to be able to return all of it back to you one day and I will. All you have to do is grant me your blessings and I'll do the rest. I am a good guy, don't ever think otherwise. I want you to feel comfortable to come to me if you ever need someone to talk to. I hope you can trust me again although I know it may take some time. I promise I won't let you down again. Thank God I had the courage to write this letter because I had to get this off my chest. I am always thinking about you no matter where I am and I know you do too. So let's begin a new, solid, and fresh relationship because it's about time. Basically, to sum it all up, I want you to open your heart because I'm coming in! (for good),

Love,
Your only son
John

P.S. You believe this is the first letter I ever wrote?

This picture says 1,000 words and I hear every word.

Part 3
The Beginning

Chapter 16
The Year 2005

J ANUARY 2005 ENTERED MY LIFE as a roaring lion devouring me. January 13, 2005, was an unseasonably warm day. I picked up the girls from school, and since it was beautiful, we played outside. We still had caller ID, and I rarely checked it; however, the house phone was ringing constantly. Before I entered the house, my cell phone rang, and my friend was hyperventilating and speaking rapidly. She asked if I had been in touch with my family in New York. It was an odd question, but I answered no. She encouraged me to call my family immediately. I ran inside the house, checked the caller ID, and noticed I missed ten telephone calls from my uncle's home in Ridgewood. When I called, my cousin Mary answered, and her voice was not as calm as usual. She managed to tell me urgently, "Caroline, John was in a very serious car accident." I thought she was referencing her brother, so my heart ached for her. She was traumatized but not crying. Mary masked her emotions well. I responded with sorrow and assured her I would be praying for her brother. I told her I would visit over the weekend. She paused and spoke inaudibly, "Caroline, it's John, your brother, not mine." My heart sank, and I dropped the phone. The girls were thirsty and hungry, so they came rushing into the house and filled the silent foyer with boisterous laughter. They stopped in their tracks when they saw me sitting on the steps with the fallen phone. I glanced at them as I struggled to pick up the phone. Mary ended the conversation and sadly told me, "The whole family is going to the hospital, and I think it is really bad, Caroline. Like really bad." My body grew numb, and I stared blankly at my two young daughters who had no idea what was going on. I called my friend back. I asked her how she knew because she had no contact with John or my family. Her cousin was one of the people waiting eagerly for John's arrival at a retreat in Boston. John was the keynote speaker.

John and I had spoken that morning as usual. He was thrilled to give his testimony to hundreds of young people. He was packing for the retreat and trip to Virginia. He was planning to propose to his girlfriend first. I was waiting for his call after the proposal. We talked more about his upcoming visit, and I told him I was preparing mentally, emotionally, and spiritually. It was a great conversation. He ended the call with another action item for me. John was a visionary and relied on me to help make his visions become a reality. He told me one day I would tell his story and help him write his book. I wrote all of John's papers in college along with Jackie's and sometimes Mary's too. Normally, I dismissed John's ideas but this one stuck. I knew in my heart his outlandish idea would transpire one day. I must have been silent for too long because my friend disrupted my thoughts. She promised to pray for my family. After I hung up with her, I called Mark. As soon as Mark heard my voice, he said, "Caroline, I am sorry, so sorry. I am on my way home, and I bought you a ticket to New York for today. It is very foggy, and there are many delays. But we will do whatever it takes to get you to John." Mark already knew about the accident and was rushing home. I told the girls John was in a car accident, but their faith was stronger than mine. They sat with me and wrapped their small arms around me and promised me Jesus was with John. They helped me pack while we waited for Mark. They were young yet so mature. Danielle packed a snack for me, but I had no appetite. Though Caitlyn was looking forward to me being lunch mom the next day, she reminded me to find another mother. They dropped me off at the airport, and Mark arranged for someone to pick me up from LaGuardia airport to drive me to Good Samaritan Hospital in Suffern, New York. I boarded the plane. As the airplane taxied off the runway and cut into the dense clouds, my mind wandered uncontrollably. I could not channel my thoughts, and obviously, my emotions were intensified. It took immeasurable effort to sit calmly in my seat without drawing attention to myself. I fought my tears. I tried to never cry in public. It was a sign of weakness, and I never wanted to be vulnerable.

I stared out the window into the clouds. I loved clouds and could spend hours making figures out of them. I kept seeing visions. My life unrolled right before my eyes, and first, I saw three young children playing the game of life. There was much laughter, and the beautiful sight made me smile. I reflected on my childhood years and treasured the memories. I kept seeing John's smile. Then the rest of our lives continued to unveil, and the reminiscences flooded my mind. John's life flashed before my eyes, and I watched him grow from the young happy boy to the grieving teenager to the drug addict to the pastor. I gazed at the clouds fixedly, and then I saw a white coffin in a large church. No! I screamed in my mind repeatedly, *No, no, no!* I shut my eyes and wept. Upon arriving at the airport, my ride was waiting as expected. I barely knew them because we met this family just a few weeks earlier. Mark's parents asked us to host them when they recently visited Virginia. They were grateful and wanted to compensate us. They were sweet, kind, and gentle. They understood my brokenness and were mindful of my tender feelings. It was a long ride, and I was eager to arrive at the hospital. When we arrived, they carried my bag and walked me into the emergency room. The hospital lobby was dark since it was after hours. From the outside, I thought no one was inside. When I walked through the revolving doors, I was immediately greeted by my big Egyptian family. There must have been more than seventy people in the lobby. Most of my family was pacing aimlessly, while others were sitting and fighting their tears. In the midst of the crowded lobby, I spotted my mother. I had never seen my mother look so helpless, despondent, and withdrawn. She walked over to me and hugged me tightly. She would not let go of me and sobbed in my arms. She told me it was very bad. My legs grew weak, and my heart sank. Jackie was sobbing and looked at me with abysmal sadness. I paused and glanced at every family member, and each one wore the same sad, helpless countenance.

One of them barely spoke but managed to provide me with the details of the accident. It was a dense, foggy day, and John was driving on the highway. There was speculation that another car hit him from behind and caused John to wean off the highway and drive onto the shoulder. There was a tow truck stopped in the shoulder lane, and John's Jeep crashed into it; however, the crane smashed John's windshield, broke the window, and hit John's head. He was immediately helicoptered to the hospital. At the emergency room, the neurosurgeon knew John suffered an extensive brain injury. John was never conscious and was already in a coma when the family arrived. The doctors did not let the family see John since he was in very critical condition. The neurosurgeon told my family that John's situation was hopeless and that his chance of survival was slim to none. Everyone wept and was in disbelief. No one was ready to accept such absurd words. Some of my family members were doctors, and though they were deeply grieved, they dowsed into their medical knowledge and refuted the surgeon. This doctor was not primed for my domineering family. The Jewish neurosurgeon was also not prepared for our strong, unyielding Christian faith, which became the driving force behind every conversation. My family had every intention to camp out at the hospital and pray unceasingly. The doctors, nurses, and hospital staff were already bewildered by our anomalous reaction from the first night. Nothing prepared them for the nine days that followed. The neurosurgeon looked past his medical expertise for a brief moment and understood our deep grievance. He was overwhelmed by our large presence. He finally permitted my family to see John.

Based on the doctor's bleak medical report, I did not expect to recognize John, and I was terrified of seeing him. Some of my family and I walked in together, and we were pleasantly surprised to be able to recognize John. He was swollen and bruised but definitely identifiable. He was intubated yet appeared comfortable. I was relieved to learn he was not suffering from pain. We were somewhat filled with hope, but the surgeon's words unnerved us. John's senior pastor and other members of his church were also in the emergency room, and they encouraged us to pray. We succumbed to lots of prayers. No disrespect was intended, but the surgeon made it clear this was a medical issue, not a God problem. There was no room for God because the medical reports were evident John's brain was severely injured with no hope of repair. Despite his grim attitude, we were convinced John would survive the accident and resume his thriving ministry. This was about God because God was always in control. The hospital waiting room became a battlefield, and we were David fighting Goliath. John's flourishing ministry was changing lives. He gave people hope when they deemed life hopeless. He brought happiness to people who struggled with sadness. He fed the hungry, visited the lonely, and loved the unlovable. Why would God stop John now? Visiting hours were over so we were asked to return the next day, though the surgeon was still adamant about John's minuscule chance of survival. My mother and I planned to spend the night at the hospital. Jackie lived nearby so she went home. My stepbrothers, John's best friend from Keswick, John's girlfriend, and a few other family members spent the night too. The night was long, and we barely slept. John's pastors stayed through most of the night and shared stories about him. They loved John and appreciated his dynamic personality. John made a difference at Jacksonville Chapel and became the change church members craved. We learned about the new ministries John created to better serve the needs of the people who were hurting. He focused on those who were neglected. John paid close attention to the people who were physically present but mentally and emotionally detached.

Like I mentioned numerous times before, John's perception was keen. And his heart was tender and compassionate. He was drawn to hurting people and was able to develop programs to help them feel loved and accepted. John's senior pastor adopted him as his son and loved him well. John finally found the father he was seeking except John did not idolize this man because he learned to only worship God. We reminisced, laughed, cried, and talked more. They moved John to a room in the ICU, so we, too, moved into the ICU waiting room. We were the only family, so we occupied the whole room. At the break of dawn, a hospital administrator greeted us warmly and was sympathetic to our situation. Her heart ached for my mother, and she discounted the hospital rules to accommodate us. She even brought coffee and donuts and made time to visit with us. My mother spoke with our new stranger friend for a few hours and shared John's story with her. The woman was startled to hear about John's journey through addiction. It struck her as odd because she didn't think we looked like a family who struggled with such issues. But she enjoyed hearing about his victory because it gave her hope. Looking back today, I realized this woman must have been struggling in her own life and personalized John's story. Therefore, she embraced hope. I confidently write this today because this woman visited with us daily and spent hours in the waiting room listening to stories. All that to say she and my mother became well conversant. My mother was friendly, outgoing, and engaging. But her heart was broken, actually shattered. She was filled with mixed emotions and thoughts were racing erratically in her mind. Yet despite her fear and doubt, she was always ready to share John's story. My mother confidently seasoned her conversations with anticipation. She was optimistic John would soon wake up from his coma and would speak to that. News about John's tragic car accident widely spread, and people from different walks of life reentered our lives. The hospital was flooded with visitors from across the country. My family was well known and established so the multitude of people was not a surprise. What we didn't know was the extent of John's ministry and the mass number of people he had reached. We were not primed to meet the families of the addicts John tended, but we were definitely impacted by them. None of the addicts were able to visit John because they were in rehab, but their parents flew in from different states to see John. They were shocked to hear the news of the accident, and there were times when we were comforting them. They wept as they told us about John's love for their children. Like us, they prayed for a miracle and refused to accept anything less than one.

We knew John was special, so we did not want to turn people away. As you could imagine, the nurses and the doctors were at a loss and could not keep up with my family or visitors. They were actually stunned at the number of people who visited hourly. Since some of us never left the hospital, family and friends brought meals, and this added more chaos to the commotion. John's neurosurgeon came from a well-renowned, orderly family, so he was not accustomed to such disarray. He truly was baffled and at times speechless. Many of my friends from Virginia drove four hours each way a couple of times per week to offer support. I was grateful for them. They experienced John, so they knew and loved him. The outpour of love and support was overwhelming but well received by my family. We needed people badly as we were hurting deeply. Our days at the hospital were long and mixed with diverse reactions to the daily medical reports. Some hours we were filled with optimism while other hours we were left with a foreboding pit in our stomachs. My extended family put their lives and jobs on hold and spent their days at the hospital. The doctors in the family tried to surrender to the hospital staff, especially the neurosurgeon, but they could not keep their distance. My stepfather flew in from Abu Dhabi, where he was working, and confronted John's doctors hourly. The neurosurgeon—I am purposely omitting his name for various reasons—continued to be shocked by our response and would go home and discuss the situation with his reputable father. In his anger one day, he eluded to the fact he never met a family such as ours. He was grappling with my family not being able to understand the severity of John's medical condition. I mentioned before John and my stepfather had unresolved issues. A few days prior to the car accident, John and my stepfather made peace. My stepfather was relieved to have reconciled with John.

I barely spoke with the neurosurgeon, but he was fully aware of my presence and was more cognizant of my silence. He knew I was John's sister because he saw me sit by John's bed daily for hours at a time. He also identified my mother and sister, but words evaded us, so we did not have much to say to him. We listened with sadness to his dismal report daily. I did not know what to expect from such a distinguished neurosurgeon, but in my brokenness, I craved compassion and sympathy. Because of the nature of his field, I respected the boundaries he set. He appeared insensitive, but my judgment was jaded by my emotions. He was being professional and honest. We did not want the truth. We wanted a fairy-tale ending to John's situation. John had been through so much, and I couldn't envision this being the end for him. I was privileged with being at the hospital continuously because I did not miss a visitor or a story. And with every visitor came a great story. It was unreal. I will share some of them over the next few pages. Each morning the neurosurgeon was astounded John lived another day. His response saddened me because I desperately wanted to witness a miracle, but his medical knowledge robbed me of such hope. He walked in on me every morning at five o'clock and waited patiently as I spoke to John. I had no idea he was listening from afar. I would hold John's hands and urge him to fight for his life. I could not tell if John heard me or not. One morning the surgeon set time aside to speak with me about John. For the first time, he did not address John's medical condition. He was more interested in John as a person because he was astonished at the stupendous number of visitors.

Surprisingly, he shared personal information and gave me background information on his family. He was forthcoming about how puzzled he was over John's medical situation. From the first day, he expected John to die and could not explain the longevity of John's life. He told me he discussed this case daily with his father. I thought it was sweet he had such a connection with his dad. I knew I was in the presence of an important person. I would normally formulate my words with caution, but my emotions were so raw that I did not make that a priority. He continued to speak to me, and I blankly stared at him. I was dying on the inside and could not find words to respond, but he kept pushing. I briefly shared John's journey with him, starting by saying, "John was a drug addict for ten years. Then he became an associate pastor." My blunt statement left him bewildered. Time was on our side because we were the only two people in John's room. He gazed at John for some time. His eyes softened, and his demeanor changed. He then looked back at me and asked, "How did John overcome addiction?" We talked more about addiction and the slim chances people have to overcome such a disease. I was not about to preach Christ to this well-renowned, intelligent, and brilliant doctor who was also Jewish. God already did not make sense to him because in his profession he was sort of a god. I certainly did not possess John's boldness in evangelism. I merely shared John's story, which I did not expect to make sense to such a man. People of high intellect who don't believe in Christ could not make sense of John's life. But I proceeded to tell him anyway because I was sharing what transpired in my brother's life. My eyes were swollen because I was not sleeping or eating, and I was weeping when no one was watching. I wanted to avoid eye contact; however, he commanded respect, and his presence was authoritative. I did not fear him but highly respected him. Nonetheless, I looked him confidently in his eyes and spoke calmly, "Jesus Christ healed John of addiction and renewed him." There was dead silence. After the words escaped my mouth, I looked away from the doctor because I was not ready to be ridiculed. Nor did I want him to mock John. I wanted him to leave the room because I wanted to cry so badly. My heart ached terribly.

Instead he stood there and finally spoke, "I now understand better. Your brother was a hero! He saved people. It sounds like John was a great man." Tears welled up in my eyes, and I fought the urge to weep in front of this strong doctor. He was a formidable force, and I wanted to exude strong faith. He slightly assuaged and briefly looked away. It gave me a chance to get a better look at him. Deep down, he was a nice man. He was in a tough position and was dealing with a family desperately seeking a miracle. He did think our family was a bit insane. In the end, people would go to great lengths to save their loved ones. He caught my eye and said, "Caroline, John is going to die. It's just a matter of days. His brain is severed in half. I respect your family's belief in miracles, but this won't be one of them. I am sorry." Oh, those words struck something within me. I will never forget them, not then and not ever. "John is going to die." It was like a knife pierced my heart. I recognized my voice but not my words.

I responded, "Doctor, there is no death in Jesus Christ. John is going to heaven and will live for eternity. The greatest miracle is the everlasting life Jesus gave us." I looked around to see who spoke those words. It was me! The doctor nodded and told me the nurses and hospital staff admired our faith greatly. Moving forward, he preferred to only communicate with me, and he planned to visit in the mornings. I understood his stance. After he left, I knelt by John's bed and wept. The floodgates opened, and I sobbed. I pleaded with John. I shook John. I begged John. I reminded him of the pact we made to live life together. I was not ready for John to leave me. I was looking forward to his visit. John's last words encouraged me. He helped me see I was broken but not beyond repair. He looked past my mistakes and loved me regardless. He was willing to set time aside to guide me. I wanted to change my life. I wanted to become the woman Christ intended me to be. I wanted to become a better wife and mother. I knew John was full of wisdom, faith, and love. I needed John. But God had a different plan for John. I settled down and joined my mother in the waiting room.

My mother was visiting with a new family whose son was recently admitted. They were a Jewish family, and their son, age thirty-four, had suffered a massive heart attack. After I walked back into the room, my mother introduced me to them. I also saw John's pastors in the room. They were the first visitors to arrive daily. John's girlfriend and my stepbrothers went to the cafeteria to eat breakfast. Jackie and her boyfriend were on their way. They picked up a few items for me. I packed for only a few days, but I extended my stay. There was a young woman sitting in the corner who had been there since the first day. She never spoke to anyone, and we presumed she was visiting another patient. The sweet hospital administrator who brought us coffee and donuts was seated next to my mother. My mother made a new friend, and this woman was gentle and tenderhearted. Then a few minutes later, a group of fifteen African-American men entered the waiting room. We assumed they were visiting another ICU patient, but they asked for Brother John Hanna. John's senior pastor exchanged looks with my mother and me and nodded no. He knew all his church members, and these men did not look familiar. My mother and I hesitated to let them visit John because the nurses restricted the number of visitors per day. We tried to reserve visitations for family members. They understood our averseness and were mindful of it, so they introduced themselves. Apparently, John conducted a weekly Bible study at a men's homeless shelter, and these men had become John's closest friends. Anyone who met John became his friend because he made each person feel that way. They were wearing John's designer suits and were carrying the Bibles John had bought them. John donated his clothes to them. My mother often wondered about the expensive suits she had bought for John because he never wore them. John's senior pastor was perplexed.

He was curious about why they referenced John as brother and not pastor. He questioned them because it irked him.

They bowed their heads and smiled. Then one of them spoke and shared how John requested they call him brother because he was not there to serve as a leader over them but serve beside them. The man continued to share how John elevated their status and never made them feel they were beneath him. He treated them as his brothers, not just by words but more through his actions. John was not checking a box by doing philanthropy. He was not volunteering so he could score points with his church or the community. As a matter of fact, John told them he needed them more. Not only did he read the Bible with them, but he dined there too. He even spent the nights when he was tired. They had a bed for John. They watched sports and spent hours discussing the plays and statistics. He wept with them. He laughed with them, and he became them so that they could rise up with him and overcome. The senior pastor interrupted the man and told them about a program John inaugurated at the church called "Overcomers in Christ." He wondered if it was the same program John ran at the shelter. The program was designed specifically for people who went unnoticed by society. Their pain ran so deep. No one saw their sufferings. Their cries went unheard. They were outcasts and had no place to go. In this program they overcame their struggles through Christ. John facilitated it weekly. From the side of my eye, I noticed the young woman seated in the corner. When the senior pastor mentioned Overcomers in Christ, she looked up and then turned away. I was so intrigued by the conversation that I did not pay much attention to her. John talked to me several times about this new program, but this was the first time I understood its magnitude. The men were aware of the program, but their fears and insecurities crippled them. They rarely left the shelter. John knew these men were not ready for a structured program, and he met them where they were. John's devotion emboldened these men. They were able to wear John's best suits, leave their comfort zone, carry their strongest weapon, which was the Bible, and venture out to the hospital. Because of John's love, they were healing. This was the first sign of it.

They respected our decision to not allow them to visit with John, but they asked if they could read the Bible with us. They read from the book of Psalms. Each one read a psalm and shared how God's Word encouraged them. When John first visited these men, they were hopeless. They had no ambitions or goals, but John gave them hope through the gospel. It was not his mission to remove their burdens but to point them to the one who could. He was dedicated to his weekly Bible study and never missed one. He brought laughter and bliss into their lives. They knew something was wrong when John did not show up. They called his church and heard the news of John's accident. After they read the Bible, each one prayed tearfully. The one prayer that still echoes in my mind was recited by the quietest of them all. He prayed, "Lord, I never knew You until I met Brother John. Even if You take him from us, we will always have You because You are the everlasting gift." Each time someone alluded to John departing, my heart sank, but I knew it was the truth. I just was not ready to accept it. Despite the nurses' restrictions, we permitted these men to visit John. I escorted them to his room. It was so hard to watch grown men sob. As big as these men appeared, they broke down and wept. They held John's hands and prayed over him. When they said goodbye to John, I wept. They knew they wouldn't see John again on this side of heaven. We walked somberly back to the waiting room. They hugged my mother and left. The hospital administrator was greatly moved by this particular visit and told my mother that if John lived, she would accept Jesus as her Savior. This gave my mother hope because she was confident Jesus would perform a miracle in this Jewish hospital so that all these people could believe in Him.

The other family in the ICU with us was also impacted and wanted to better understand Jesus Christ and His role in John's life. My mother's hope exploded, and she was excited to honor John by sharing the gospel. She knew this would gratify John, and she couldn't wait to share this news with him when he woke up from the coma. This family was desperate for a miracle and was willing to believe in anything to save their son. After hearing about John's journey, the mother believed. She claimed she felt unexplainable peace whenever she heard the name of Jesus Christ. She recognized the psalms from when she prayed in the synagogue, but they touched her differently on that day. I honestly thought she was delusional. I had never witnessed anyone accept Christ quickly and without hesitation. But she did, and it truly was a beautiful moment of someone totally surrendering to Christ. I was not in the right state of mind to fully embrace the moment because my heart was too broken. And I knew it was going to shatter further. John's story changed people's lives, and this was one I witnessed and recorded in my mind. I was too brokenhearted to rejoice because I was more focused on John. But this mother genuinely and openly received Jesus Christ as her Savior. She prostrated in the middle of the waiting room and prayed in the name of Jesus Christ. John's pastor seized the moment and prayed over her. They joined hands and prayed for some time. She was tearing up, and so was Pastor Matt. My mother was also deeply touched, and it affirmed her confidence in John's story being a miracle. She kept telling the hospital administrator that John would live. It really did not help that this administrator was waiting to witness the miracle. Without exaggeration, within an hour, the family's son woke up from his coma. I was definitely more attentive to that miracle. But it was someone else's miracle, and I was happy for them. Of course, I wondered if we, too, would witness a miracle. The mother ran down the hallway, praising Jesus. Her voice carried, "I believe. I believe in Christ, my Savior!" They later moved her son into a room one floor above us. My mother encouraged her to share the good news with her son.

This born-again woman shared the news with each person she met in the hospital. Soon the entire hospital perceived my family to be miracle workers and prayer warriors. They visited us in the waiting room so that we could pray for their sick family members. It was comforting to be in constant prayer, but fatigue and exhaustion consumed me. Though this family was moved to a different floor, the mother visited us throughout the day. They soon became part of our family and were genuinely concerned about John. The rest of my family showed up, and my mother shared about our day. They loved hearing more about John's ministry and his impact on people. John's neurosurgeon heard about the homeless men who had visited, and we talked about it the next morning. He continued to be fascinated by John's ministry as it unfolded. He openly admitted to me that John had become a special patient to him. John's brain continued to swell, and my stepfather coerced the surgeon to perform surgery. The doctor was enraged but complied with the request. He scheduled the surgery for Friday, January 21, 2005, at 10:00 a.m. We had two days before the surgery, and people continued to visit from all over the country. I especially enjoyed the visits from people we had known since our childhood. We had not seen them since our father had passed away in 1988. They were disheartened over John's serious condition. Even the grown men, my father's dearest friends, wept when they saw John.

Jackie was scared, but like me, she put up a good front. Because she did not spend the nights at the hospital, she debriefed me every morning. We rarely had any privacy, so we whispered and tried to divert attention away from us. We were deeply loved, and though we greatly appreciated the outpour of ardor, we felt smothered at times. Jackie wanted to discuss something that was heavy on her heart. She and John recently argued a lot over her "unequally yoked" relationship with her boyfriend. John liked him but did not think he would be a suitable husband for Jackie. She refuted his argument and stood her ground. Jackie barely cried and was struggling to keep her tears at bay. She asked me if God was punishing her. Jackie thought God was punishing her because of what she perceived to be a sin. She thought God wanted to take John away from her because she was not living a godly life and refused to heed John's advice. Meanwhile, I was struggling on a different level. I made a commitment at the beginning of the year to seek God. I did not expect Him to respond this way. I wanted God to reward me for choosing Him, but I felt I was being punished. I was inherently focused on myself, and I made this situation all about me. I was not thinking of John. I realized I was not listening to Jackie until I noticed she was staring at me, waiting for a response. I felt sad for her and took the liberty to divulge the wisdom John imparted to me. I helped her understand God was not punishing her. I was always grateful for the guidance of the Holy Spirit because the words I spoke to Jackie that day truly came from God, not me. I am a person of words. I could speak them even if I did not believe them. Jackie was relieved of that heavy burden after that. She was astonished to learn of the topics John and I had discussed. I was forward about his concern over her spirituality, but he was confident she would find her way. That also calmed her.

Jackie was hurting deeply, and I could see it in her eyes. She asked me if I thought John was going to die. I paused for a long time. She kept pushing me for an answer. I finally said, "Yes, John will die." That was not the answer Jackie was expecting. She looked away, and tears welled up in her eyes. Then we locked eyes. No words were exchanged, but I felt the pendulum of her somber mood.

"Why do you think he will die?" she asked dismally.

Once again, I did not accept my own words, but I knew they were the truth. I continued, "John is ready to go to heaven. His mission is complete. And he wants to go. John does not want to stay here." She looked around the waiting room and briefly glanced at each family member and looked back at me. She fought back her tears because she noticed my mother was watching us closely.

She said, "Everyone is going to be sad, very sad." Despite the family's persistence that John would live, Jackie believed me and was melancholy from that day. She wondered if we should stop the upcoming surgery and let John rest in peace. But we knew that was an uphill battle we were not prepared to fight. It was a welcome distraction to be surrounded by the extended family in the evenings. We did not want to be alone and engaged in different conversations. My family was entertaining, and the five-course meals contributed to the ongoing chaos we brought into the hospital. We generously shared our food with the nurses and hospital staff. Some of the family started to spend the night because they did not want to be apart from John. They spent a lot of time with him, talking to him. It was challenging to visit John in the evenings, so I reserved my time for the early morning time slot. Jackie continued to go home. She was not wired to handle such commotion. It irritated her tremendously.

John and I welcomed chaos, but Jackie rejected it. She made me promise to call her if anything happened. People visited until midnight, and the hospital administrators rescinded the visiting hours for us. I think they liked having my family at the hospital, even though we brought disorder. They've grown to love and admire John just from the stories they were hearing about him. My family hung on to every word and insisted on hearing the stories they missed. Jackie and I had our favorites. Jackie loved the one about the disabled young man who worked at Nyack College cafeteria. When John went back to college, he enrolled in Nyack. Regardless of how hectic John's schedule was, he made ample time for his meals. And he enjoyed cafeteria food, so he dined there daily. He became acquainted with this special young man who wiped down the tables. John immediately noticed him and started to converse with him. This became the highlight of this young man's day. He looked forward to John's lunchtime. John carved out time from his hectic work schedule to visit with this man. John made him smile. John was patient with him and moved past his speech impediment. He gave him time to express his opinions. They discussed many topics, but they both discovered they were passionate about sports. The shy, withdrawn man found a new purpose for his existence and looked forward to his afternoons with John. John never missed a lunch visit and for three years, these two strangers became best friends. They always ended lunch with a high five. One of John's college friends shared this story with Jackie at the hospital, and it stayed with her. John and Jackie were tightly knitted together and were inseparable. But they were very different. They touched people's lives in different ways, but Jackie grew to appreciate John's tenderness and compassion for the people who went unnoticed. Jackie wanted to hear this story many times, so she kept narrating it in her gifted and animated way throughout the night. I, too, enjoyed hearing it just as much. But there was another story that touched me more.

It was about the young woman sitting in the corner of the waiting room since the first night we moved to the ICU floor. Because of our traumatic experience and the number of visitors we had daily, we barely paid attention to her. Though we noticed her, we assumed she was visiting another family so we left her alone. She was quiet and appeared sad. As the days passed, my mother appreciated distractions, so she wanted to learn more about the mystery woman in the corner. Day after day, the woman was sitting in the same chair with her head down and hands folded in her lap. We became very concerned about her because she was alone. She arrived promptly at 9:00 a.m. and left at 6:00 p.m. My mother urged me to talk to her. I walked over to her and tapped her gently on her shoulder. She reluctantly looked up, and it was evident she was crying. Her eyes were swollen and red. Looking deeper into her eyes, I saw a young woman who had lived a hard life. I asked her if she was okay. She looked up at me with sadness and told me she was waiting to see John Hanna. My jaw dropped for various reasons. First, she had been there since the first night but never approached us. She just sat there quietly and kept to herself. Second, I did not recognize her. Nor did anyone else. I was fascinated by the different people John knew and had impacted, so my first question was, "How do you know John?"

She responded softly, "John saved my life. He was my best friend."

Again, everyone was John's best friend! Every person who visited John in the hospital was his best friend.

She shared her story. "My life was a hot mess, and I was so ashamed of my lifestyle. I felt worthless and had no purpose. I started to attend John's small group, 'Overcomers in Christ,' and he shared his struggles with drug addiction. But the focal mission of the group was how God redeemed John. I wanted what John had. He made a mistake, openly admitted it, was no longer shamed, and was living an abundant life. He was the happiest person I knew, and I coveted his joy. No one ever took interest in me, and I often went unnoticed in crowds, so I was taken aback by John's attentiveness. I was not ready to be noticed but welcomed John's pursuit. We had a great conversation. He was easy to talk to. I felt I was the most important person in the room. Then he asked me the tough question, 'What do you do?' I didn't want to tell him the truth. But there was something deep in his eyes, and I felt he already knew the answer. I could not lie to him because he exuded sincerity coupled with compassion. I was in dire need of both. I was embarrassed by my profession. John's nonjudgmental reaction eased me, and I unleashed vented-up sensations regarding my demeaning job. John's eyes were kind and tender, and he placed his arm on my shoulder. He gently told me to walk away from the job, and he promised to help me find a new one. John spent hours filling out job applications with me. He went with me to apply in person. John prayed with me and for me. I had never experienced Jesus Christ until I met John. I was lonely, destitute, and in great despair. But after attending the small group, my life shifted, and I was filled with hope. I was given a second chance. John assured me I was beautiful and deeply loved. I never heard such words before. A woman like me could only feel cheap and worthless, but John's words saved my life. I was born again. Like John promised, I landed a new job. I am not making the astronomic salary I was in the previous job, but I feel like a million dollars. John promised if I gave my life to Jesus Christ, I would experience the abundant life he was living. He kept pointing me to the Lord. I wanted to tell John he was right. I wanted to tell him that God had answered his prayer and that I had gotten the job he had helped me applied for. I tried calling him numerous times, and he usually responds promptly without delay. I was surprised he never called back, so I contacted Jacksonville Chapel, and they sadly told me about the car accident." She paused and wept. "He was my best friend, the first person to believe in me and give me a second chance at life."

I maintained my composure as best as I could. I asked her if she wanted to see John. She insisted I accompany her. We walked into John's room. She walked over to his bed, held his hand, and cried until there were no more tears. It was emotional and heart-wrenching. She thanked him for not labeling her the way society did, for believing in her when no one else did. With quivering lips, she whispered softly, "John, thank you for making me feel worthy when I felt worthless, for helping me when I was helpless, for loving me when I was unlovable, and for giving me hope when I was hopeless." She hugged John and would not let him go. She looked up at me and asked, "Is John going to be with Jesus in heaven?" The question was filled with hope and joy but intermingled with sorrow and sadness. I nodded yes, though I did not want to believe it. She responded, "Heaven is lucky to have him. I've never met anyone like him before. It's like he is not real." God brought the beauty of ashes in this woman's life. Her story was one of my favorites about redemption and hope. John entered her life and embraced the good, the bad, and the ugly. He was genuinely concerned about her lifestyle and walked the extra mile with her. Because of John's love, her entire life shifted and moved in a new direction.

Remarkably, John did not need to witness her transformation to believe. He surrendered her to God and had faith she was going to be fine. Her story did not end here. This beautiful redeemed woman met one of John's recovering addicts, and they married one year after John's car accident. The addict's story was also a great redemptive story. The man was young, hopeless, depressed, and addicted to drugs. John visited him frequently in jail and would lie down next to him for hours. The man was not motivated and fell into dejection. John would sit quietly with him and promised not to leave him until he was ready to get out of bed. Despite John's hectic daily schedule, he set time aside for this important visit. John read the Bible to him, and the gospel became his lifeline. God's Word became the most effective healing power in this man's heart. The Holy Spirit ministered to him and changed his heart. The young man found new hope deeply rooted in Christ. When he was released from jail, he went through rehab and overcame his addiction. Like many people, he had setbacks, but with John's support, he overcame them. These broken hearts were mended through God's healing power, and they became one. It was the most beautiful love story woven together with redemption, hope, and love because one person had believed in these people. But the story did not end there. This beautiful couple paid forward the gift John had given them. They took over "Overcomers in Christ" and continued John's ministry. John was the gift that kept giving. It was the truest testimony of a person who served the Lord and not himself. I knew I was never going to see this woman again, but she certainly left an impression on me. We embraced for a long time before we left John's room. I introduced her to my mother before she left.

After she exited the waiting room, visitors started to show up earlier than the previous days. It was day seven, and family and friends were anxious, fatigued, and terrified. My mother urged me to share this young woman's story with the family, and they were in complete wonderment. As John's ministry unfolded daily, we were enthralled by the magnitude of his life-changing work. Had John died the first night, we would never have learned about his ministry. John was an ordinary man who became extraordinary because of the power of Jesus Christ. Our days were long but filled with heightened emotions and commotion. Some of my family frequented the chapel and spent hours praying. Jackie and I could not pray, but often we went with them. Throughout the day we had visitors from the twenty-plus Coptic churches in the New York area. Most of the priests visited and prayed for John. We also had visitors from the Protestant churches, both Arabic and American. Suffice it to say that we had a gargantuan number of visitors per hour. When I saw John alone, I seized the moment and slightly shut the door. I stood over John, and a wave of emotions swept over me. I knelt by his bed and pleaded with him one more time, "John, please don't leave. You're helping people, and they need you. I met the people you impacted, and they love you. The family needs you, and I know you enjoy being with them. We are all here now. Everyone is here for you. You would never believe the number of visitors you get every day. I was looking forward to your visit and was ready to heed your counsel. Please don't go. This can't be real. Please stay, John. Please." I whimpered, Then I unleashed my emotions, and my tears soaked John's blanket. I hugged him and would not let him go. I kept repeating, "Please, John."

As I began to settle down, I looked up, and John was standing before me. I shut my eyes tightly and opened them, but John was still standing there. He was an illuminated vision of light. He stood before me, and my mouth was widely agape in astonishment of the beautiful apparition before my eyes. I was mystified and gawped at John until his voice interrupted my baffled mind. "Caroline, please let me go home. I am ready to be with the Lord for eternity. I completed the work the Lord set before me. Please let me go."

"Noooo!" I screamed back at John, but it was my inner voice yelling at him because my mind became a war zone. Perhaps I was hallucinating. I was fatigued, exhausted, despondent, and terrified, and so many emotions consumed me. I could not let John go. I shook him and pleaded with him. I continued to hear his soothing voice say, "Caroline, do the Lord's work by pointing people to Jesus

Christ. Share my story. It must be told. I was afflicted but never crushed, perplexed but never driven to despair, struck down but never destroyed, faithless but faithful, hopeless but hopeful—all because of Jesus Christ. He never fails."

I retorted with frustration, "I don't have your boldness. I don't want to preach and tell people about God. I don't know how to tell people about Jesus. I am not like you, John. I will never be like you or Daddy. You have to stay and tell people your own story."

In his parting words, he said, "Caroline, Jesus will help you tell my story because it's not just mine. This is everyone's story. Everyone needs hope, and it is only found in Christ. Never lose hope, Caroline. Don't take your eyes off Jesus. I promise He will never forsake you. He loves you. I am going now to be with Him, and we will meet again soon. Please let me depart in peace."

Oh, my heart, my heart was throbbing so badly. I reached out to touch John, but he was gone. He vanished just like that. I looked back at the bed, and he looked so peaceful. The neurosurgeon walked in and startled me. I looked up, and my face was sopping with tears. He gently nodded, and it was obvious he, too, was sad. I dug deep into my mind to find words to speak. For the obvious reason, my mind was wasting away, but I managed to utter, "John is leaving very soon." The neurosurgeon looked away, but I kept searching his eyes for any glimpse of hope.

Instead he concurred and said, "Yes, Caroline. John is going to die within a day or two. As promised, I will perform surgery tomorrow morning, but it won't be too long after the surgery. Please know I am thinking of you." He was a stranger to me but was the only person I could speak to. I followed him and returned to the waiting room. Surprisingly, my mother was alone. I sat in the chair next to her and looked at her. I had never seen my mother look so afraid. She was a strong woman who weathered many storms, endured many trials, but looked frail at the moment. This was tearing my mother apart. She aged over the past few days and appeared gaunt. Her eyes were sunken, swollen, and red. She looked back at me, and we sat quietly for a few minutes before I broke the silence and said, "Mommy, please go tell John he may depart in peace."

She looked perplexed. "Leave and go where?"

My palms were sweating. My heart was beating so rapidly I thought it was going to bust out of my chest. I mustered up the courage to tell her she needed to let John go. "Mom, I think John needs you to let him go," I said. Did those words just leave my mouth? How could I tell my mother to let her son die and be fine with it? She suffered through John's years of drug addiction. It had only been three years since John recovered from addiction, and she was enjoying the renewed John.

She processed my words, and she dumbfounded me with her response, "Do you think if I told God he may take John from me, He would let John live like He did with Abraham and Isaac?" The story of Abraham was one of the best stories of the Old Testament. Abraham waited a long time to have a son. Then God tested Abraham and asked him to offer his son as a sacrifice. Abraham obeyed. As he was about to sacrifice his son, God spared Isaac's life. It was a great story, and my mother wanted to make it her story too. She was suffering, and I needed to be sensitive. She was losing her mind, and I needed to understand. I could not dismiss her thoughts and desperate cry for God's intervention.

"That is a possibility," I replied gently but then continued, "I think God's plan for John's life is different. Back in October, John told me he was ready to go home. It did not make sense to me at the time. Nothing John said recently made sense, but Mom, I think John wants to go heaven. He always said this was not home. Heaven was his home." I even told her about the conversation John and I had regarding his marriage proposal and how he felt in his heart it was not God's plan for him to be married. She knew John was on his way to propose because the police found the wedding ring in his pocket, covered in blood. For one hour I disclosed to her my recent conversations with John. She gasped. She was not aware of John's spiritual growth and intimate relationship with God. It pained me to keep talking, but I needed to fight this one last time for John. For years I fought for John but this was the final battle. I looked back at the times I stood in the gap to protect John. Memories flooded my mind, and I vaguely recalled one time when we were in the apartment in Staten Island and the superintendent's son robbed us. He was not aware that John, Jackie and I had stayed home from school because John had pretended to be sick. He entered using his father's key and stole my mother's jewelry from Egypt. We were in the room we shared, and we heard the door unlock, so the three of us ran to the foyer and saw him from afar. I was eight years old, John was seven, and Jackie was six. John was excited and thought the young man was coming over to entertain us. But I knew something was odd, so I held John back against his will. John was unruly, and it took strength to control him. He was physically bigger and stronger than me, but my protective instincts kicked in. I shoved him and Jackie into my parents' room, and we hid under their bed until the young man took what he wanted and vacated the apartment. I then called my parents. John was scared and was grateful for my protection, and he learned to trust me more after that. This was one of the many ways I fought hard to protect my brother.

I spent years fighting for John, but this battle was the most important one. I had to do this for John. I set my feelings aside. I looked at my mom and said, "John is ready to go to heaven, Mom, and he needs you let him depart in peace. God wants to bring John home. He belongs to the Lord, and he's finished all the work God gave him to do. He completed his mission."

She nodded no and continued to nod incessantly. "No, Caroline, no, I don't want John to die. I want him with me, even if he never spoke or walked again. I don't care about that." Her pain was deep, deeper than mine. She was his mother, and I was telling her to be fine with John dying. It was absurd, so I remained patient and calm.

"Mom it would not be fair for John to live that way. And you wouldn't be able to handle it." I explained that John would die regardless, but it might give John more peace if she let him go. I coerced her until she caved. We both walked to John's room and stood by his side.

She held his hand and looked at me. "He is so beautiful." John was handsome. He was a perfect combination of my parents. My mother started to cry as she opened her mouth, and her words poured out. "Okay, John. Okay, you can go to heaven, John. You may leave in peace and be with Jesus, John. I know you want to be with your father too." John's body juddered, and we both got startled and jumped back. We thought he was waking up, so I ran to get the nurse. She took his vitals and confirmed there was no change in his status. John was still in a coma, but we were convinced he must have heard my mother. Even the nurse agreed. We wanted to believe it so badly, at least for my mother's sake. I was not going to let anyone take that away from her. I knew right at that moment that John was leaving soon. I think my mother felt the same because she fell into my arms and wept. I wanted to give her all the time she needed, so I asked the nurse to give us privacy by not allowing visitors or hospital staff into the room. We did not say much and sat in silence except for our muffled cries. The rest of the day was somber. We continued to have many visitors, meals, and conversations; however, the mood definitely shifted, and everyone was gloomy. We were anxious about the surgery the next morning, but most of the family doctors insisted that the neurosurgeon proceed as planned. The neurosurgeon made a surprise appearance. The family knew he was avoiding them, and they were content with his decision because he rattled them with his candid prognosis. He discussed the surgery and was very matter-of-fact. He wished the family well and told them it was a privilege to have met them. He admitted he learned so much from our family. He seemed sincere, and I knew the family welcomed his kind words. He was basically bidding the family farewell.

The next morning on January 21, 2005, I woke up at three o'clock in the morning, sat by John's bed, and watched him for hours. I did not utter one word but observed his chest rise and fall. His swellings went down, but he was still bruised. He appeared to be sleeping. I looked up to see if he was watching me from above. I had watched too many movies of people who had flatlined and had undergone out-of-body experiences. I had so much to say to John, but instead I gazed at him until his neurosurgeon walked in. He was more nostalgic than the night before. He once again for the hundredth time shared with me his reservations regarding the surgery but promised to comply. He guaranteed its failure but felt he had nothing to lose. John's medical case was hopeless, and his brain was beyond repair. He was candid and did not want to season it with false hope. It was evident he was sympathetic, but he was not my friend. He was my brother's neurosurgeon. My mind wandered to the miracles Jesus had performed. God created John's brain, and I knew He could repair it. Why didn't God want to prove this neurosurgeon wrong? God was in control over everything, but why was He distant? I must have spaced out because the doctor walked over to me and laid his hand on my shoulder. "Caroline, I don't mock your faith by any means, and I admire your strong belief in God. John's brain is irreparable. I wish I could save your brother's life. He is someone worth saving and fighting for, but there is nothing I can do for him. Please take your time. I can postpone the surgery if you need more time with John." He walked out. I ran after him and told him to proceed as planned. I returned to the waiting room, and I saw that it was more crowded than any other day. Many had spent the night, but the room was quiet. Breakfast was served, but no one ate. One of my cousins suggested we pray, but no one was able to utter a word, so he prayed while the rest listened. He prayed for the team of doctors and for my family to accept God's will regardless of the outcome. Honestly, I hated hearing that because I knew what God's will was. I was not ready to accept it. My mother admitted to me the only reason she willingly let John go the day before was that she wanted God to spare his life like He did with Isaac. She retold me the story again about Abraham and Isaac. She thought that if John came out of his coma, all the nurses and even the surgeon would witness the most amazing miracle.

My mother was losing her mind and rightfully so. I was falling apart but wanted to be mindful of my mother's pain because I knew it was far deeper than mine. She stopped talking when she saw the doctors wheeling John down the corridor. We all ran outside the waiting room and encircled John's bed. It was obvious the medical team was sympathetic to our feelings because they stopped and gave us time. Some of the nurses had tears in their eyes but were trying to compose themselves. Amidst the crowd, I saw John's neurosurgeon. He looked in my direction, our eyes met, and he just nodded. I understood from the exchange of looks that the end was upon us. We anxiously waited for hours, and in the meantime, visitors flooded the waiting room. Many of my friends from Virginia drove four hours in the cold, blustery January weather to spend a few hours with me. I enjoyed their visits and welcomed the distraction, but anxiety crippled me. Soon thereafter, the neurosurgeon informed us that the surgery was over and that John was in the recovery room. He was surprised John had survived the surgery and explained the procedure in great detail. He was more patient and gentler than usual. The purpose of the surgery was to release the pressure in John's brain so that the swelling could go down. He was not hopeful the surgery would save John's life but was surprised the swelling decreased a bit. We were able to visit with John. They had shaved part of his head, and he had a bandage wrapped around his skull now. Jackie and I visited with him alone for an hour. A few family members were in and out of the room, but Jackie and I stayed for the duration of the night. We were talking about all the visitors John had and how he would have enjoyed seeing them. John loved people.

Jackie reminisced about our childhood years. While she was speaking, I stared at her. She looked back at me and asked, "What?"

I hesitated but knew I needed to tell her. "Jackie, I think you need to spend the night." She did not want to hear such words.

"Why?" she asked.

Sadly, I replied, "This is it, Jackie. This will be John's last night with us."

"*What?*" she screeched.

I was stoic and poised but dying on the inside. "Jackie, I don't think John will live another day. I actually believe John is already gone. He left us." I hesitated to share too much with Jackie because she was in agony. Jackie was always the strongest and never wore her emotions on her sleeve. John meant the world to Jackie, and I knew this was maiming her. She was struggling spiritually and would not have understood what my mother and I had witnessed over the past few days. If I told Jackie about the vision I saw, she would think I was delusional. I was not ready to be berated. Despite my fragile condition and weakened state, I was confident about what I had witnessed. Jackie agreed to spend the night. She didn't even harp on her concerns about where and how she would sleep. She was anxious and terrified of how the next few hours would unravel. Sure enough, Jackie and everybody else spent the night. Mark and the girls drove from Virginia, but Mark sent the girls to spend the night at my cousin's house. We barely slept through the night. I paced back and forth down the corridor. I conversed with some of the nurses who were working the night shift.

As the nurses prepared to leave in the morning, they embraced me and said goodbye. Some of them opted to stay for the day to be with us. I was touched by their gesture. They frequently visited John. I walked in when one of them was whispering in John's ears. She was startled when she saw me. It was obvious she was embarrassed and felt the need to explain. "Caroline, I was saying goodbye to John. I told him I believe in his God because I witnessed pure love these past nine days. I asked Jesus Christ to be my Savior last night, and I was sharing the good news with your brother. Because of John, my life is filled with hope, peace, and joy. I never knew I was missing them until now. I don't need for John to walk out of this bed to witness a miracle because I believe in my heart Jesus Christ is my miracle. I never spoke with John, but I love him so much. I admire his heart for the people who were hurting deeply, people like me. I am sorry for your pain but happy for heaven's gain. Thank you for sharing your brother with me." We embraced, and I wiped away her tears. I assured her that John would have enjoyed meeting her, and she responded perfectly when she said, "He and I will meet one day in heaven." She told me she planned to stay until the end. She was a sweet and gentle woman who provided outstanding medical care for John. She was a phenomenal nurse who kept him comfortable. After she walked out, Mark, Jackie, and Amy walked in. Mark appreciated and loved John well. John often told me Mark was one of the few people who never judged him, even when John was at his worst. He never felt threatened by Mark. He was grateful for Mark's financial support regardless of how much John squandered the money. Mark was fatigued from the past nine days. He drove back and forth several times, and he cared for our daughters during the time. Mark was also emotionally drained. He was sad to lose John. He genuinely loved him and highly valued his witty sense of humor. We stayed in the room for some time, watching John.

Amy was heartbroken. She knew John was going to marry her, and they talked extensively about their future life and children. We briefly chuckled about John's insane wedding idea. He wanted to get married at our ranch in Middletown. He thought it would be beautiful for him and Amy to reenact Adam and Eve's relationship in the garden of Eden. They would be naked just as God had created Adam and Eve, and they would come out of the bushes, meet at the altar in the garden, and get married. It was bizarre, irrational, and impractical but humorous too. John would laugh as he described his idea in fastidious detail to us. And we would chime in and laugh with him. Amy laughed at his absurd idea but adored John's lighthearted outlook on life. Amy was laughing one minute and then bawling the next minute, reflecting on her dream as it passed by, never to become a reality. We, too, cried with Amy as we watched John slowly drift away. My mother entered the room and started to cry when she noticed our teary eyes. My mom knelt by John and kissed every part of his body. She kissed his feet, his legs, his arms, his hands, and when she got to his head, she said, "John, my beloved son, go home." We all stood in the room, sobbing relentlessly. A few seconds later, John released his hand and rested it by his side. This abrupt movement scared us, but we knew he was not waking up. We left my mother and Amy alone with John.

Mark, Jackie, and I walked back to the waiting room, where our extended family was. They barely slept, were anxious and irritable. My heart plummeted to my feet, and I was scared to death. I knew what was coming but did not want it. I looked over at Jackie and told her it was going to be very soon. It was snowing outside, and I was surprised when more friends from Virginia arrived at the hospital. They visited with John and wept. They did not stay long because of an expected snowstorm. Mark's parents and his brother also came to visit John, and they were sad. My mother-in-law cried because she loved John very much. She enjoyed his visits to their home, and he always made her laugh. They went to see John, and my mother-in-law came out of the room, sobbing. She hugged me warmly and softly spoke into my ears, "I am sorry, Caroline. I am so sorry." They had a family friend who was an exceptional and well-renowned doctor. He told my mother-in-law that John was going to die very soon. He, too, was crying when he hugged me before he left. Tears trickled down my face. My lips were quivering, and I was shaking. Jackie was sitting with Mark in the corner. She did not want to speak with anyone because she was apprehensive. Her boyfriend did not spend the night but arrived early to be with her. I sat with Mark, and he held me for a long time as I sobbed in the waiting room. I told him I did not want John to die. He did not know how to respond. In all honesty, I did not know how he should respond. There was nothing he could do to stop God's plan. No one could. Mark's quiet and calm spirit comforted me for a brief moment until Amy hysterically ran into the waiting room and yelled, "John … John is leaving us. Hurry up!"

Everyone ran rapidly down the corridor into John's room. The room was filled, and everyone was hysterical. My uncle adored John. He loved him like a son. He was watching the monitors and repeatedly said, "John is going to be fine. This is nothing. John is fine." We believed him because he was a cardiologist. John's blood pressure was dropping rapidly, but my uncle insisted John was fine. The nurses were rushing in and out. Then they stopped and waited outside quietly. My mother's brother and my father's younger brother were sobbing and shook John a few times. Jackie and I were standing beside John's head, stroking his hair. Amy and my mother were holding John's hands. Mark was standing beside me. One of my closest friends from Virginia had stayed the night, and she, too, was in the room. My cousins were there too, and they were crying. My aunts were frazzled and terrified. It was the craziest day in the ICU. We surrounded John's bed and kept watching the monitors. There were so many sounds, and we could not distinguish between the many machines. The snow was coming down rapidly. It was dark and gloomy outside, which darkened John's room further. All my male cousins were there. John was a brother to them. Some of them were crying, while others were pacing frantically. Two of them were doctors, and they watched the monitors closely, which made people more anxious. My uncle continued to assure us that John was going to be fine. He said that it was a minor setback but that John would overcome it. But the one nurse I had seen earlier with John stayed in the room with us. She glared at my uncle a few times, but her glance softened because she was perceptive enough to recognize his denial. She stopped refuting him and allowed him the time he needed to let go. John's body jolted a few times. His breathing slowed down, and he flatlined. John Kamal Hanna passed away peacefully on January 22, 2005, at eleven thirty in the morning. Be still my heart!

The wave of emotions that swept over me at that moment could not be inscribed in words. I knew it was coming, but when it hit, I wanted the earth to swallow me up. I was crushed in spirit. I was shattered. I was hurt. I could not utter a sound. The eruption of the wailing sounds in that small room was piercing and painful, but I was too numb to react or respond. The room was full of people, and yet I felt so alone. My mother fainted, and some of my family members took her out of the room. She was in bad shape. Jackie and I laid our heads on John's chest.

My mind became a violent war zone, and the battle was intense. My inner voice was the only sound I heard, and I was yelling at God. I was shaking my fist at Him. How could God do this to me? I yelled, "I changed my mind. I want John back. Don't take him. Leave him." Tears trickled down my cheeks. "Please, John, don't leave me. Please stay." I tuned everyone out, and it was just God and me. I screamed at God. "Fine, if you want John, then take all of us *now*. Take us with John. End this world now. You have the power over this earth, and You can end it today. I can't wake up tomorrow without John. End the world, end the world, end the world, please, please, please!"

In this moment of great distress and sadness, I heard a very soft and gentle voice. I did not know where it was coming from, but I know I heard a small, still voice. Obviously, I thought I had lost my mind. But I heard the voice over and over again, "Keep your eyes on Me. I love you."

"No, I want John back" I screamed. The voice would not go away. I knew I was still lying on John's chest. Mark had his arms around me. He asked me if I was fine because I was not moving. I think other family members left the room, but I refused to move. Time froze for what seemed like an eternity. I wondered if anyone else could hear what I was hearing. Or was I hallucinating? I kept hearing that voice say, "I love you. Keep your eyes on Me. I am your hope." I definitely thought I had lost my mind.

God sabotaged my plan for life, and I was devastated. My

dreams were shattered. I slowly released my grip on John, looked up, and saw him from afar smiling peacefully at me. John was in heaven. I knew it in my heart. Everyone vacated the room. Mark and I were the last ones to join the rest of my family in the waiting room. My mother was lying down in a hospital bed and was heavily sedated. I could not approach her because I did not know how to comfort her. I was pacing back and forth. My phone was blaring with text and voice mail messages, but I could not answer or respond. I walked to the nurses' station, but I did not understand why I felt compelled to head that way. The neurosurgeon was seated among the nurses with his head down. I did not realize he was still in the hospital, so I was surprised to see him. The nurses were crying but stopped short when they saw me. He, too, looked up at me. He barely spoke, "I could not leave." Tears dribbled down his cheeks. He was actually crying. "I was fortunate to have been John Hanna's doctor, and I hope I could be half the man he was. I am very sorry for your loss." He walked around the nurses' station and warmly embraced me.

I softly uttered, "Thank you for taking the best care of my brother."

Hours later we were still in the waiting room. We could not leave the hospital. My mothers' condition worsened, and she needed time to recoup. Family and friends were making phone calls to notify people about John's death. We were receiving countless calls. My friends from Virginia whom we met through my cousin John F. did not even know of John's car accident. They were shocked and saddened to hear of his departure. John loved this particular group of friends. We went to their eccentric and entertaining New Year's Eve parties in Virginia. During the summer of 2004, John attended their father's funeral in Virginia. Their father was Muslim, and their mother was a Christian. As John and my cousin John F. Hanna were heading back to New Jersey after the funeral, he walked over to say goodbye to me. John's goodbyes were never brief. He stood with me as he watched this family grieve their father's loss. He told me he loved them so much. He loved them enough to want to share the gospel with them so that they could come to know the Christ we love and serve. Then he implored me to share the gospel with them. I just looked back at him and thought, *Have you lost your mind?* How would I approach them and initiate such a conversation? I rolled my eyes, pushed him along, and told him I didn't preach. I constantly explained to John the difference between him and me. John had more confidence in me and saw an innate boldness I did not feel. He recurrently told me that I was bolder than him and that one day I would lead many people to Christ. I begged to differ because I knew I did not possess impudence or genuine concern. They were the friends John planned to visit in January. I envisaged these thoughts while I was on the phone with one of our friends from that group. She was crying, and she had so many questions regarding the accident. She was in disbelief over the tragic news of John's death. I abruptly told her that John had urged me to tell her that Jesus Christ loved her and wanted her to follow Him. I didn't know why I blurted such words in the midst of this conversation. Because she was crushed and vulnerable, she received my words without query. I could not believe I spoke such words.

John passed away at eleven thirty in the morning, and my family vacated the hospital at seven o'clock in the evening. Mark and I went to pick up our daughters. As soon as I entered my cousin's house, Caitlyn asked, "Mommy, did John go to heaven?" I tried to fight back my tears because the girls learned in their Christian school and at church that going to heaven was good. But I was sad, and I cried. She and Danielle hugged me, sad to see me fall apart. I was weary, hungry, and despondent. I had barely eaten for the past nine days. My girls had never witnessed me grieve and were not prepared to watch their happy sunshine mother become a dark cloud. We spent the night at my uncle's home in Ridgewood and barely slept. The next day my family returned to Staten Island to start the funeral preparations. My mother continued to be heavily sedated. She could not accept John's death, and she was deteriorating. John was an associate pastor at Jacksonville Chapel, but my mother insisted we have his funeral in the Coptic church in East Brunswick, New Jersey. The senior priest of that church grieved John because he adored him. He told my mother that it would be an honor to have John's funeral at his church. This caused an upheaval because John was not a practicing Copt, but I won't dwell too much on that. Though I had much to write about this, I knew it would disappoint John and not honor God.

John prayed for unity among churches and denominations. The priest was not concerned about the problems it caused him because he learned and grew from John's example. He was grateful to hear about John's ministry and the effect he had had on people. The funeral was set for January 25, 2005, at St. Mary's Coptic Orthodox Church in East Brunswick, New Jersey. We still had two days to prepare, but we needed the time to decompress and finalize the preparations. People continued to visit, and their company was well received by my family. It was hectic at times, but the commotion kept us sane and motivated. As we finalized the funeral arrangements, Jackie and I insisted on having an open casket. We wanted to see John one last time.

Most of the family was against this decision, but I fought for it and won. The funeral home was a long way from Staten Island, and the long journey was tiresome and daunting. My mother was not well enough to attend the wake so some family stayed behind to care for her. Danielle and Caitlyn also stayed home with my mother. We drove for a few hours and finally arrived at the funeral home. It was dark, gloomy, and cold. The funeral home was situated on a corner street, and there was ample parking, but no space was big enough for the number of people who showed up. They gave the family one hour for private viewing. The family argued profusely about the open casket, but I could tell they wanted to see John one last time. One of my younger cousins wanted John to wear his favorite New York Yankees baseball cap. John was dressed in one of his best suits and was wearing the baseball cap to cover his half-shaved head. He lay peacefully in the casket as though he was just sleeping. The whole family—men and women, young and old—encircled the casket and wept bitterly. For one hour we wept, wiped our tears, and cried again. No one was ready to let John go. It was sad. After the hour ended, the doors opened, and the family stood for hours receiving condolences. Jackie, Amy, Mark, and I were in the front row and were accompanied by my stepfather, uncles, and male cousins. My stepbrothers were young, sad, and scared, so they stood behind us with John's best friend from rehab and his cousin. My twin cousins and stepsister were also seated in the second row. My aunts and female cousins were seated in the third row. I was flummoxed to see most of our high school friends, even the ones we did not stay in touch with. Jackie and I hugged each one and allowed them to take time to reminisce and mourn. There were people we had not seen since my father's funeral, and we gave them time to talk. So many of my friends from Virginia drove up, and I was surprised to see them. I was grateful for each one because I knew how difficult it was for them to commute back and forth, especially in the snow.

The multitude of people came from the twenty Coptic churches in the New York and New Jersey areas, the Protestant churches from Pennsylvania, New York, New Jersey, and Boston, men from the homeless shelter, families of addicts, Jacksonville Chapel, Keswick, childhood friends, Jackie's friends, and some of the nurses from Good Samaritan Hospital. It was a grueling and harrowing experience, but we felt loved. The funeral home director notified me of the number of people wrapped around the funeral home. He tried to make room for them because of the blistering temperature, but he couldn't. The director told me they never had so many people for one person. He was speechless. After several hours we were ready to go home. The funeral home director gave us another hour for private viewing, and despite our chronic fatigue, we stayed. It was hard to walk away. It was the last time we would see John. I kept hugging and kissing him. I held his hand. I shook him once, hoping for a miracle. It took time to peel me away from the casket, and as I walked away, I kept looking back. "John, please come back." I kept saying these words in my heart. We drove back to Staten Island in complete silence. My cell phone rang constantly, but I stopped answering. I had no words.

The next morning my family and I were in shambles. Everyone was in disarray. Jackie, Amy, and I were finalizing our eulogies. Amy's family arrived in the morning from Connecticut to follow us to East Brunswick. John's pastors arrived shortly thereafter and were emotionally drained. I read my eulogy to Mark, and when I looked up, he had tears in his eyes. Mark rarely cried, so his tears melted my heart, and I broke down. I did not want to cry. I wanted to be strong. I was trying to keep it together. My mother was already in bad shape, and I knew the next few hours were going to be the toughest hours in her life. Her eyes were distant; her mind was absent. She was delirious and could not cope. My heart ached for her, and I knew there was nothing I could do at that moment to ease her pain. She needed to walk through the suffering. God was with her, but she felt alone. Every family member was grieving. We were initially in denial and could not believe John had died. I kept repeating, "John died. Oh my, John died." The words shocked me each time I spoke them. John's friend from rehab asked me, "Did John really die?" He was angry. I definitely did not want to be angry at God. Many years later I realized I was indeed angry. I was angry that John was hit by a reckless driver we had never met. I was angry at the renowned neurosurgeon who could not repair John's brain. I was angry the young man who suffered the heart attack lived and John did not. I was angry at God because He could have saved John but did not. The pain of loss consumed me on that morning, and I was frustrated and helpless. I always had a solution to every problem, or I thought I did. On the way to the church, which was a long and quiet ride, I bargained with God. God could still raise John from the dead the same way He raised Lazarus when his sisters wept over their brother's death. As a believer in Christ, I knew I had to accept John's death as God's will. We rode in the car in complete silence, and scripture flooded my mind. I kept hearing the words John recited often.

> There is wonderful joy ahead, even though you must endure many trials for a little while. These trials will show that your faith is genuine. It is being tested as fire tests and purifies gold—though your faith is far more precious than mere gold. So when your faith remains strong through many trials, it will bring you much praise and glory and honor on the day when Jesus Christ is revealed to the whole world. (1 Peter 1:6–7)

I struggled to see the joy in this suffering, and I further wrestled with my faith. I could not believe God would do this to my family. He had already taken my father away, and we suffered his loss greatly. But who am I to question God? Well, I did. God understood my intense anguish. He was able to handle my temper tantrum.

We approached the church, and I was stunned by the mass of cars in the parking lot. There were a few charter buses too. I heard that a few churches, especially the distant ones, had rented buses. Mark pulled up in front of the church, and my mother began to weep when she saw the hearse. She did not attend the wake the night before, so this was her first glance at John's casket. My stepfather and her brother escorted her out of the car and did not let her approach the coffin. She broke down, wept bitterly, and yelped in great anguish. Her waves of expression were natural but frightening, especially to my daughters, who had never attended a funeral. They were close to their grandmother, but they only experienced her joyful spirit. She was a different person now, and it terrified them. There was very little we could do to calm my mother down. We would be foolish to expect my mother to be stoic or strong. We let her be, and it was excruciating. As we walked in, the funeral director asked me if we wanted them to bring in the flowers. He had two vans filled with flowers. I looked at him with a blank stare. I had no response. He kept talking, and I looked through him and focused intently on the hearse. I wanted him to open the coffin, but he sadly looked at me and nodded no. In the meantime, we agreed to empty one van because there were too many arrangements. The church was overflowing with people. I was overwhelmed with the number of people. All the Coptic priests in the area were also in attendance. There weren't many deacons because they were too disheartened to participate in the service. Some of John's closest friends who were also deacons were sobbing. The priest from Virginia embraced me as I took my seat in the front pew. He had another funeral in Virginia, but he postponed it so that he could attend John's funeral. I was touched by his sweet gesture.

All my friends from Virginia drove up for the funeral. The church was packed. I choked up when I saw the homeless men. I understood the complexity in arranging for their transportation, so it meant a lot to see them again. I was surprised to see John's nurses again because it was a long distance from Nyack. The next few hours were awful. We took our places in the front pews, and a few of my male cousins and John's friends were the pallbearers. They proceeded down the aisle behind the priests and deacons. As the coffin approached the front of the church, my mother lost it. Her condition spiraled downhill rapidly, and a doctor friend sedated her. The sedation calmed my mother down, but she appeared lifeless. The Coptic funeral was a long service, and the hymns were melancholy. There were several eulogies. John's pastor embodied his extensive ministry, and most people were stunned to hear about John's pastoral care and the extent of his ministry. Most of the Coptic priests were ashamed of the way they judged John. One told me later that John accomplished more in his three short years than he did in his twenty-plus years before that. The bishop who delivered the final eulogy referenced the story of Lazarus in the Bible. It reminded him of Jackie and me. To be honest, I mulled over the fact Jesus could still raise John like He raised Lazarus. I looked at the coffin and wanted John to wake up. Well, that did not happen. John's life was an eye-opener to all the people attending the funeral. They were in disbelief over John's radical and drastic spiritual transformation. Unfortunately, most of them did not have the faith to believe a person such as John could change. It was easier to relish in gossip and rumors than to see God work in a person's life. As the funeral came to an end, everyone in the church was weeping. Most of the attendees proceeded to the cemetery except my mother. She passed out and could not attend the burial. Some extended family and my daughters stayed behind with my mother. My daughters were terrified at this point, and a big part of me regretted they had attended the funeral.

My uncles, aunts, stepfather, Jackie, and I rode in the limousine to the cemetery. We were trying to leave the church, but people surrounded our car to offer condolences. Some of our family friends were touched by John's life, and they expressed their sentiments. They wanted to learn more about his journey, but we did not have the time or heart to discuss it. The ride to the cemetery was silent except for everyone's inaudible cries. When we arrived, it was chaotic and hectic. It was crowded, and it felt claustrophobic. There was snow on the ground. It was blistering cold, and people were emotional and needy. We could not support other mourners because we were about to bury John. We were dying to say the least. I could not fathom John was gone forever. One of the Coptic priests prayed the Lord's Prayer followed by John's senior pastor's farewell. Everyone congregated around the casket. As the prayer ended, my uncles bawled and shrieked for John. It was gut-wrenching. Their screams were high-pitched and painful to endure. I knew my uncles adored John, and this was hard for them. Because I cocooned into my own world, I neglected to see the effect this was having on my extended family. John's burial plot was adjacent to my father's. My parents purchased their burial plot through the Coptic church in the early 1970s. My mother never thought she would bury her son there. I peered at my father's headstone, and the blood drained from my face. I felt weak and got down on my knees. I knelt by John's casket and laid my head on it. I could not breathe. I placed my hands on the casket. I looked up into the sky, desperately wanting to see John one last time. I was surrounded by so many people, but I felt alone.

My heart was broken. I was hurting so badly I could not feel anything. I drowned out other people's cries and looked down to where John would be descending soon. I had no choice to but let go. He was already gone. I made eye contact with the gentleman working at the cemetery. He was overwhelmed with the swarm of people and was pacing aimlessly. We locked eyes for a few seconds, and I reluctantly nodded my head. That was my cue for him to start lowering the casket. As the family watched the casket descend, their cries elevated to a piecing wailing sound. The suffering was intense. I watched the casket descend slowly and felt my world collapsed. I was in such agonizing pain that I could not be comforted. I was watching them bury my brother, whom I loved with all my heart. I could barely tolerate the pain; it paralyzed me. My body stiffened, and my heart was shattered. I felt this was the end for me. I was coming to the end of myself. I soon learned that as we come to the end, there is a beginning. I further learned that we don't come to the end of ourselves once. It's an ongoing practice until the ultimate culmination. John taught me God authored our story, and as each chapter ended, a new one began. God's story had a happy ending because it was the beginning of eternity. As this chapter in John's story ended, his new life in heaven, his ultimate destination, began. The beginning starts at the end.

Chapter 17
First Version

THE BEGINNING STARTS AT THE *End* was ready for publication in 2007, two years after John passed away. My heart was not settled, and I had many sleepless nights. I wanted to honor John's final request to write his book. But something disturbed me, and I could not pinpoint the source of my anguish. I could not publish the book. One night I dreamed of John, and he kept saying, "No, Caroline, don't." I knew I was doing something wrong. I felt it in my heart, so I set the book aside for a brief time. I eventually reread the book and immediately understood the root of my apprehension. The first version of this book did not honor John, and it definitely did not revere God. I was avenging John's life and appeasing my anger. I was angry, but I was blind to that feeling. Anger was one emotion I never wanted to feel because I knew it would control me. I did not allow myself to express anger. In the past I walked away from situations to avoid it. At times, I admitted I was wrong only to avoid confrontations that could leave me angry. John asked me to write his story of hope. He never asked me to defend his honor. He did not want people to know how he was judged, condemned, and ridiculed. He surrendered his sufferings to the Lord, and God healed John. John wanted his book to fall into the hands of people who were hopeless, lonely, sad, and struggling. He wanted to tell them that there was hope. He was in the deepest pit, and now he's in the highest place, heaven. He wanted people to read about his Savior, who never abandoned him. John understood the purpose of his addiction. It was an ugly part of his life. It was the worst chapter in his story, but God used it for His glory. John's words in my dream resonated with me, "No, Caroline, don't."

My anger specifically targeted church and Christians, basically my own people. I described how they mistreated John in revolting details. The exposure would have been disgraceful. While I thought I was writing John's story, I was judging and condemning others to esteem my brother. John said, "No!" The first book was going to hurt people because I was hurt. "Hurt people hurt people." I never forgot John's discerning words. Another powerful insight John shared was his reflection on the Samaritan woman. After she met Jesus, she put on Christ and was transformed. Because of her life-changing encounter, she shared Christ with the same people who shunned her. They judged her because of her sinful life, but she responded with love. She did not withhold the gift she received. She paid it forward. John did the same. He proclaimed the good news to the people who ostracized him. When they rejected him, he responded with love. That was the purest form of love. It was the message John wanted people to read. It was summed up in one word—*love!*

The 2007 version did not communicate love and hope. I wrote my own account. It was not my story to tell. It was God's story of redemption, restoration, and hope. Like John enlightened me, God authored our stories and weaved our lives together for a reason. I was honored to write John's story, but it was marred by my false perception of God's objective. It was no accident John asked me to write about his journey. There was a far greater purpose than I envisaged. But I was not prepared for God to pursue me through this endeavor. Regardless of how far I ran away from God's reach, He found me. He met me in my darkest places. While I thought I was writing for others, the message was ultimately for me. It took years to accept this because I thought my life was intact. It was easier to label people like John because his addiction was palpable. I believed John's story could give hope to addicts or people who struggled in recognizable ways. But I was exempt. I excused myself. I knew this book had to be published. But I did not want to write it anymore. It exposed things about me I was not ready to deal with. It was easier to walk away. And that's what I did. I walked away. Hence, the battle began, and it was grueling. I was stubborn and did not relinquish control easily. God pursued me through my toughest trials and tribulations. I came to the end of myself many times yet persevered by my own fervor. My strength became my greatest weakness. I lost hope in God, people, and myself. I fell into the deepest pit. The beginning of my journey started when I came to the end of myself.

Chapter 18
Life after John

ONE YEAR LATER I WAS still mourning John's death. I went through life but did not experience it. I refused to love people deeply, especially my family because I did not want to hurt if I lost them too. I shut down, and it affected my relationship with people. It impacted my marriage and my ability to mother my children. I had nothing to offer and was not allowing myself to heal. I was losing myself, but I was too proud to reach out for help. I tried grief counseling but did not reap its benefits. I barely slept and ate. When I finally slept, I dreamed of John. One dream brought closure to John's death, but the grieving period was incessant. I could not stop crying on that one particular day, and memories inundated my mind. I was home alone after I dropped off the girls at school. I was looking through my childhood family albums for hours. The memories were so vivid, and I just could not let go. I was not reading God's Word for comfort as I was taught to do. I was not good at memorizing scripture, so I could not resort to my memory. But I kept hearing a specific verse in my mind. I was not familiar with it but recognized it from the book of Psalms. "The Lord is near to the brokenhearted and saves the crushed in spirit" (Psalm 34:18).

Those words did not bring me comfort. My heart was broken. My spirit was crushed, and the Lord was not near. I felt abandoned and hurt by God. I guess I was one of those Christians who liked God when life was good. But when my world turned upside down, I questioned His goodness. I shut the photo albums and sat in silence. All I kept asking was, "Why, God? Why?" I was completely exhausted and took a nap. When I slept, I dreamed of John. This was the most vivid dream of John I had experienced.

He was lying in a bed, and I was standing over him. He was in a hospital bed, but there were no doctors, nurses, or visitors. I nudged him a couple of times, but he did not wake up. I heard a soft voice yet the words were loud and clear. "I took John to spare him. He battled addiction but remained faithful to Me. Daily he chose Me over his desire for drugs. He put Me first." Then John rose from the bed, and I saw the image of the "Faithful Servant," the one that hung in my bedroom. I saw Jesus embrace John and heard Matthew 25:21, "Well done, good and faithful servant. You have been faithful over a little; I will set you over much. Enter into the joy of your master" (Matthew 25:21).

I then heard the same words spoken at John's funeral by several people, but I had never embraced them until I heard them again in my dream. "Truly, truly, I say to you, unless a grain of wheat falls into the earth and dies, it remains alone; but if it dies, it bears much fruit" (John 12:24).

People referenced those words because they knew John's life would bear much fruit. As I tossed and turned, the apparition vanished, and I heard these final parting words, "John's story is my story of redemption, restoration, and hope." I woke up and knew I was commissioned, but I filed it away. Life was full of interruptions, and I was not able to buckle down and focus intently on this calling. I struggled to write or share a story I did not believe in my heart. I've always been told I would be a successful salesperson or politician because I could sell anything to anyone. But what most people did not know about me was I could not sell something I did not believe in. I knew how to be pretentious, and I had definitely mastered the art of being ostentatious; however, I still could not write this book. I witnessed John's life unfold and grasped the miracles in his life. I observed him walk from darkness into light. I knew he was redeemed from the pit and was exalted to the highest place. But this was all head knowledge. My mind and heart were not interwoven. They were at war. I did not just want the head knowledge. I wanted to believe it in my heart. I did not understand the magnitude of this desire. I only looked forward to experiencing the end, the victory, the triumph, and all the good, so I rushed my journey.

I decided to move on because it's what I did best. I fall and get back up. John's death was the first hurdle to overcome, and so I did. I moved on and accepted John's death, or I thought I did. I knew he was in heaven and reminded myself he was happy. One of my many setbacks was my mother's grief. I felt sad for my mother. She was deteriorating rapidly. It pained me daily to hear her cry. She struggled to make sense of God's plan, which was not aligned with hers. Her only comfort was John overcoming addiction and spending his last few years helping the helpless and giving hope to the hopeless. Another source of comfort was furthering John's ministry. We founded the John Hanna Foundation, and the money we raised was donated to addicts who could not afford to pay for rehab. We worked directly with Keswick. We also continued the Christmas homeless ministry John began. We went to Penn Station on Christmas morning in Newark and gifted the homeless with hats, scarves, blankets, coats, and a warm breakfast. We sang Christmas carols, read the Christmas story, and prayed with them. I began to understand the true meaning of Christmas through the eyes of these broken people. We also built the John Hanna Library that my brother had envisioned for Keswick. I previously mentioned John's desire to renovate and expand the library at Keswick. He did not have the funds, but we never doubted the library project would be completed. Sure enough, a few years after John passed away, we raised the money and exceeded John's vision. One of our childhood friends donated most of the money to make

John's dream a reality. John's life was fruitful, and it was the gift that kept giving.

I continued on the path I set for myself and recalled John's final words to me. He imparted his wisdom to me for many months prior to his fatal car accident. I stored these conversations in my mind and slowly recovered them. I put his words into action. In the foreword I briefly mentioned a shameful moment in my life. I made a terrible mistake, and it affected several people. At the time, I recognized my fault, but pride blinded me. John was not interested in the details, but he criticized the way I handled the situation. I harbored bitterness but masked my anger. I never learned how to manage my anger or deal with it, so it was easier to hide behind it. John cared about my heart and understood anger would corrode it. My problem was I preferred to be ruined by words of affirmation than truth or criticism. Truth forced me to get out of my comfort zone and face my grievance against others. John urged me to apologize. He told me I would never be judged for what others did to me. I would only be judged for my response. And my response did not stem from love or forgiveness. It was rooted in anger. After John passed away, I became vulnerable and maybe a little humble. I mulled over his words and knew he was right. It was hard to apologize, but I finally did. It lifted a heavy burden I did not realize I carried.

John's advice flooded my mind, and I wanted to heed each one. He encouraged me to join a Bible study. He specifically recommended the book of Romans. It was his favorite book in the Bible, and it was the one that transformed his life. I did not know where to look, so I put it on the back burner for a short while. In the meantime, I resumed volunteering at the school my daughters were attending, Trinity Christian School. It was their first year at Trinity, and the transition was challenging. The girls were previously attending a Baptist school and were happy there until the school board and administration challenged our Coptic faith in 2004. When John visited that year, he liked the school but did not appreciate their stance. He encouraged me to find another school. When we were forced to choose between our Coptic faith and the school, we made the tough decision to leave. We finished off the year and moved the girls in 2005. Trinity was a great community, but it took time to adjust. I started to substitute teach in 2004 before moving the girls. They were still young enough to make friends, but their greater struggle was the academic program. Caitlyn was in the second grade, and Danielle was in the fourth grade. We had a great start to the year, but then when John died in January 2005, things shifted a bit … or maybe a lot. I had no choice but to push through, so I got involved again. I signed up to chair the father-daughter dance, and one of the PTO members called me. Ironically, she only had sons but was assigned to this event. We laughed about it, and then she proceeded to apologize for not reaching out sooner. She explained she was busy her with her Bible study homework. It piqued my interest. She was attending Bible Study Fellowship at Centreville Baptist Church. I had never heard of BSF before, so she described it, and I was mesmerized by it. She asked if I was interested in joining the following year since they were wrapping up that year. Without giving it much thought, I immediately responded yes. Then her next few words astonished me. "Great, Caroline! Next year we will study the book of Romans." I gasped. I knew it was meant to be, and I was excited to study the book that had transformed John's life.

I appreciated BSF's structure and their way of studying the Bible. As I delved into this book and studied each verse, I understood what John was trying to convey to me. I could not believe I was saved because Jesus died on the cross for me. I had heard the news throughout my childhood years, but I had never embraced it. I spent most of my years trying to be good to gain favor with God. I better understood my struggle with sin and the battle between the flesh and spirit. God gave us the Holy Spirit to be our helper. I learned about God's grace, an undeserved gift because God loved me so much. It was refreshing to focus more on God's unconditional love than His wrath. I opened my heart and asked Jesus to come into me. But there was a problem, and of course, hindsight is perfect. Though I spent nine months in scripture, faithfully attended each class, and diligently completed my homework, I still did not grasp the message. Something was missing. I desperately wanted to walk in John's shoes so I could experience the peace he described. In his last few words to me, John said if I truly had the peace of God, nothing in the world would rattle me. Not only was I completely rattled, but I was falling apart. I just did not know it. Nor did I show it. I kept it under control for many tiresome years. I walked away from BSF with dogma, but my heart was not softened. Though I received Jesus in my heart, I set boundaries and limited Him. It was blasphemous but true. It was sad I could not trust God with my life and felt the need to control everything, especially my spiritual life. I read books on how to change myself, but in the end, I reverted back to myself. It was daunting. I continued on my journey to complete my action-item list.

My top priority was Danielle. John's words resurfaced because I noticed my little miss sunshine darken and lost her glow. John was concerned about the way I mothered Danielle. He even read a book on the relationship between mothers and daughters so he could wisely counsel me. I would love to receive credit for the radical change in my dealings with Danielle, but it was evident God was with me. I did not know why I struggled with Danielle, and it hurt my heart deeply. I loved her so much, but a mother's love could be toxic. I was molding her into a person she was not equipped to be. I failed to realize God had a different route for her. I was tough on her, and at times I hurt her with my words. Without evil intent, I shamed her in front of her peers over test grades. She never answered me back rudely, never rolled her eyes, and was always polite and respectful. One of the worst carpool drop-offs happened when she was in the sixth grade. It was early in morning, and we carpooled with another family. She wanted to tell me something but was scared, so she was hesitant. She had to tell me because she needed my signature on her math test. When she told me her grade, I reprimanded her harshly, and she just took it all in. Her eyes welled up with tears. As she exited the car, she looked back at me and gently said, "Have a nice day, Mommy. I love you." Caitlyn was in fourth grade and glared at me while exiting the car. She was upset for her sister.

I pulled into the school parking lot and cried. I could not believe what I was doing to my sweet, gentle, and loving daughter who was always a ray of sunshine. I noticed Danielle was not as cheerful and bright, but I dismissed it. I knew she was struggling with John's death but more with my grief. After I cried my eyes out and felt like the worst mother in the world, I wrote her a note and taped it to her locker. I already ruined her morning. Her Bible teacher noticed her sad disposition and comforted her. The young Bible teacher called me, and I met with her in the afternoon. She expressed concern about Danielle and rightfully so. It was humbling because this teacher was not a mother but exuded more wisdom than me. My mind was racing with rapid responses to defend myself. I really thought I was the perfect mother and had motherhood figured out. To her credit, she was not questioning my mothering but focused more on Danielle's God-given talents and how each student was unique and excelled in different ways. She encouraged me to focus on Danielle's strengths and help her overcome her weaknesses with patience. She loved and admired Danielle and told me I have a treasure in her. I listened quietly, and her words mimicked John's words. Mark and my mother repeatedly told me the same thing, namely that I was too tough on Danielle. Mark was concerned I was going to strain my relationship with her as she grew older. After my meeting I picked up my carpool and asked Danielle if she read my note. She responded yes, and that was it. I guess I was expecting a more enthusiastic reply, but I let it go.

She was obviously still hurting, and I needed to give her space.

When I looked in my rearview mirror, I could tell Danielle had been crying all day. I stifled my cry but was definitely sad the whole ride home. Most of my struggle was in my mind, and my thoughts consumed me. I convinced myself I was an awful mother. It was a pretty day, but Danielle wanted to watch television instead of playing outside. I opted to not ruin her day further, so I backed off. I was getting dinner ready while she watched television in the kitchen. I also kept my eyes on Caitlyn while she played outside with our neighbor's son. I was focusing more intently on Caitlyn because she was constantly talking to this boy about Jesus, but he was Muslim. His mother expressed concern. I never stopped Caitlyn but watched from afar. The distraction delayed me from realizing Danielle was watching *Gilmore Girls*, a show I did not think was age-appropriate for her. I sat with her and calmly asked why she was watching a show she was not permitted to. Danielle was not willfully disobedient, and I knew she was not acting out. She just looked over at me and said, "I just really want that mother-daughter relationship Lorelai and Rory have. They are so close, and Rory can tell her mom anything without fear." Tears trickled down Danielle's face. My heart ached so badly, and I had two options at that point. This was it for me. Either I would restore my relationship with my daughter, or I would sever it. She and I finished watching the episode. I had never seen it before and was able to filter through the drama and discover what Danielle was coveting. I turned off the television and looked at Danielle before I spoke to her. She looked so young, vulnerable, and hurt. There was deep anguish in Danielle, and I did not know how to tap into it. There was so much pain in her eyes. She was only twelve years old but was carrying a heavy burden. I opened my mouth, and the words gushed out, "Danielle, I hurt you, and I am sorry. God created you perfectly, but I was trying to adjust His workmanship. I was wrong. You are beautiful, smart, kind, and gentle. You have a heart for Jesus, and He shines through you. You will always be my little miss sunshine. You can trust me, and we will get through anything together. You are always safe with me. I promise. I love you so much, and I'm honored to be your mother."

I did not know what to expect as I humbled myself before my daughter. I was not sure if she was going to tell me she hated me, couldn't forgive me, or it was too late. Instead she threw her arms around me and rested on my chest for some time. Then she looked at me and said, "I have always dreamed of this day. I want to be able to tell you anything. I have so much to tell you, and one day I will. It makes me feel safe to know we can get through anything together." As time passed—days, months, years—Danielle was more transparent with me. Since that day, she felt safe with me. After we hugged and cried, she vented about her struggles with friends at school. It made me sad she was trying to navigate through some rough waters on her own. She was struggling with one particular friend who had invited her last year to her birthday party and then omitted her from the guest list this year.

It made sense when I picked her up from carpool why she had been crying. Her friends and the other girls were in the next section with their sleeping bags, going to her friend's birthday party. Danielle wept in my arms. She did not know why she wasn't invited. She even gave her friend a birthday gift in school because she thought there was no party. I asked her if she would like me to speak to her mother to get a better idea of what occurred. I encouraged Danielle to think carefully if this was a friend worth investing in. She decided she wanted me to talk to the mother. A few days after the party, the mother and I met over coffee, and we had a great conversation. She shed light on a few things Danielle did and how they had affected her friend. The mother was gentle, insightful, encouraging, and helpful. I discussed with Danielle how to build stronger friendships. We talked through a few of her weaknesses and how to overcome them. I applauded the way Danielle welcomed constructive criticism and grew from it. Her friend left school for a few years because of an illness. It was challenging for her to maintain friendships, and her return to school after a few years was difficult. The girls were in high school when this friend returned. Danielle matured and grew much in wisdom. She was one of the very few students who warmly welcomed back this girl. She helped her transition back into the school environment. I am happy to write this friend has become a lifetime friend of Danielle's and they are best friends today as adult women. Danielle was astute at twelve years old and knew this friend was worth investing in.

In the meantime, our mother-daughter relationship exceeded *Gilmore Girls*, and Danielle's dream became a reality. The words Danielle spoke to me that day after we watched *Gilmore Girls* stayed with me. She wanted to feel safe with me. But nothing prepared me for the burden Danielle carried for years. When our relationship began to evolve, Danielle was preparing her heart to share a deep, dark secret that haunted her for years. John knew something was wrong and had an uneasy feeling. I don't think he even knew the depth of Danielle's suffering. It took Danielle eight long years to muster up the courage to tell her secret. In the meantime, it was internally destroying her. I knew in the third grade Danielle was struggling, but I attributed it to the issues we were dealing with at the Baptist school. She did not handle their rejection of our Coptic faith well. The girls were not being treated fairly by some teachers. Only one teacher fought for my family, and I will forever be indebted to her. The girls were being excluded from parties and other social events. It was hurtful, and I fought hard for their rights. But there was too much pushback. It deeply saddened me because my father emigrated from Egypt to escape Christian persecution. I never expected to deal with such an issue in America. I knew something good was going to emerge from it. And it did. I transferred the girls to Trinity Christian School, and it was a better fit for my family. I thought Danielle's struggle was the school situation. It was a major issue, so I never discounted it. But Danielle's suffering was much deeper and darker. I got Danielle's permission to share this major life event, so bear with me as I share what shattered my daughter's heart.

We started to attend the Anglican church when the girls were in high school because Caitlyn was spiritually struggling in the Coptic church. Mark and I listened to Caitlyn as she boldly approached us. Danielle was not pleased with this decision and was initially resentful. She reluctantly attended the Anglican church and constantly bickered with us. Then one Sunday the pastor was preaching about Rahab in the Bible. His sermon was profound, insightful, and impactful. Danielle wept through the entire sermon. After church, she, Caitlyn, my mother, and I went to Tysons Corner Mall. Danielle tried to stifle her tears, but I noticed them. My mother was concerned too. We kept asking her, and she said the sermon touched her heart. Her answer did not satisfy me, and I knew there was something deeper but did not push her. I tossed and turned all night, concerned about Danielle. I worked at Trinity, but I left before the girls once Danielle started to drive. I felt uneasy, but I was getting work done before my upcoming trip. I was taking a few days off to be with my sister in New York for her first baby's birth.

It was in the middle of the afternoon, and I was sitting at my desk. I worked at the front desk, so I was constantly interrupted. They were blessed interruptions. The headmaster taught me that. Danielle walked into my office area and shut the door. Her eyes were swollen and red. She stood there without uttering a word. Her lips were quivering, and she was shaking. I asked her as gently as possible, "Danielle, what is wrong, sweetie? Something is not right." Her face was pale. She had circles under her eyes, and she was so thin. It was the first time I got a good look at her. I knew the junior year was academically challenging. She was taking several advanced courses and had many sleepless nights.

She started to cry as she said, "Mommy, I have to tell you something, but please don't get mad because I am scared to tell you." My heart rate accelerated, and I thought my heart was going to jump out of my chest. What could she possibly tell me? Was she pregnant? But how? I knew she was not sexually active, but I did not want to be naïve, so I prepared myself to hear those words. I kept thinking, *Bring it on, and we will deal with it.* "Mommy, I was sexually abused for a few years since I was in the third grade." Everything stopped. My heart stopped beating. My breathing stopped, and the world stood still. She continued, "Please don't tell Daddy, and I am sorry for being a bad girl." I hugged her and would not let her go. She fell into my arms and wept uncontrollably. I was grateful for my coworker who lived in our basement. She was wonderful to my daughters and loved them a lot. She recognized Danielle's recent decline and was praying for her. She immediately knew something was wrong and came to my rescue so that I could have private time with Danielle. I assured Danielle that I was not mad and told her that she was not bad. It was not her fault. Her offender convinced her she was a bad girl and it was her fault. I wanted to cancel my trip to New York. She insisted I be with my sister because it was her first baby. Danielle was thoughtful, and she always put other people's needs before hers. Even during her worst crisis, Danielle was more concerned about Jackie's needs. I fumbled for words but promised her we would get through this. I had no idea how. I had so many questions, but I knew she needed time. I also needed time to process. I was dying. I never felt so helpless. How do I have hope at a time like this? Will my daughter survive this?

I told Danielle I would tell her father because he loved her and had the right to know. She was ashamed of him and did not want him to view her differently. Mark always reassured the girls of his unconditional love. Without preparing me, Danielle blurted out the identity of the offender, and I was shocked. He was someone I knew well. But I bore the blame, and the guilt overwhelmed me for years. I should have been more attentive to my daughter's pain. She was screaming out, and I was too deaf to hear her cry for help. I thought we lived in a safe world where nothing bad happened to my family. The pain I was experiencing at that moment was excruciating, and nothing could comfort me. Danielle went back to class, and I returned to my desk. I was disoriented and didn't know how I survived the next few hours. My office knew something was wrong but gave me time and space. My sweet coworker did not pry but told me she knew of a perfect counselor if we needed one. I took the name and number. I called the counselor immediately, and she consoled me. I was crying, but she reassured me everything would be fine. She promised God would use this one day in Danielle's life for good.

She encouraged me to tell my husband immediately so we both could help Danielle. She warned me that it would take years and that I would have to be patient. She reminded me it took Danielle years to come forward. After I hung up with her, I called Mark. I would have waited, but I was leaving for New York and wanted him to comfort Danielle. Just like me, Mark was shocked. He asked if I knew the identity of the person. He told me not to tell him. Mark still does not know who the offender was. He knew he would not be able to control himself. He and I buckled down and helped Danielle start the long healing process. Though Danielle started counseling, she declined rapidly. It was agonizing to watch her suffer. She developed a love-hate relationship with Mark and me. She loved us and needed us terribly but secretly blamed us for her trauma. I had nightmares for months. I woke up every morning tormented by my nightmares because I would hear Danielle screaming out for help. Danielle was becoming rebellious. She violated school rules and made senior year very difficult for both of us. I was always caught between her and the school administration. She was not getting into major trouble, but it was enough to cause issues. She also made things tough at home, and there was constant friction between Mark and her. She was not getting along with Caitlyn either, and Caitlyn could not wait for her to leave for college.

The year 2013 was the beginning of a long, arduous season for my family. There were other serious family issues brewing, but it was hard to focus on them. Danielle's situation consumed me completely. The only thing I knew was I could not make it about me, and I devoted myself to helping Danielle heal. The counselor was the best gift that emerged from this situation. She was instrumental in Danielle's transformation. It took years, but she was faithful and never gave up on Danielle. I am forever indebted to this beautiful woman who loved my daughter well. She encouraged me to pick a verse and pray it faithfully over Danielle. I started to pray, "And I will give you a new heart, and a new spirit I will put within you. And I will remove the heart of stone from your flesh and give you a heart of flesh" (Ezekiel 36:26).

Danielle's heart hardened more. I was a bit perplexed because I thought God's Word had power and expected an immediate change in Danielle. Well, I learned God's timing was different than mine. He had a different agenda for Danielle, and it was going to take longer than I had anticipated. One of the consolations I had was God's foreknowledge. He knew this was going to be part of Danielle's journey. And He would control the outcome and use it for good. I did not have the power to expedite the process, so I waited, and it was a long wait. Senior year was coming to an end, and there were two catastrophes that troubled Danielle. The first came at her from a male classmate who sent a mass text to other boys in her class, demoralizing her. The words were hurtful in light of her situation, which no one knew about. Some of the boys who received the text were upset. They brought it to the attention of the administration. The school was ready to expel this student, but Danielle put the boy's needs before hers. She requested the school not expel him and allow him to graduate. They respected her decision, and Mark and I did as well. The second issue involved some very close family friends Danielle cherished. They were having their own family drama but masked it for years. Unfortunately, we were not aware of their problems until it was too late. Danielle was the first to detect the issue because of her keen perception. This was a sensitive matter. However, their issues poured into our family, and it was perturbing. This situation distressed Danielle. Despite the heavy burdens Danielle carried, she excelled academically and was accepted early into her first college choice, James Madison University.

She went away to college and thrived. She became an ambassador at JMU and succeeded in all her endeavors. She continued counseling, exposed her sexual abuse, tackled her issues, and had the best college experience. She owned her faith and grew closer to God. Her heart began to soften. She graduated on the dean's list from JMU in May 2017 and was accepted into George Washington University's accelerated nursing program. My prayer for Danielle of Ezekiel 36:26 was answered four years later in 2017. She was a new creation with a new heart and spirit. Danielle was completely transformed. I humbly watched God work in her life. He used that ugly time in her life and made it beautiful. Only He takes the good, the bad, and the ugly and makes them beautiful. Danielle knew Rahab was a prostitute in the Bible and likened herself to that woman. Her offender shamed her and blamed her for his wrongful behavior. He made her feel like Rahab. But God met Danielle in her deepest pit and reminded her that Jesus Christ came from the lineage of Rahab. Though Danielle does not preach with her words, she exemplifies Christ daily to others, especially to me. As she came to the end of herself, it was the beginning of Danielle's new life. Once again, I was knocked down but refused to stay down. I pushed through.

Caitlyn was next on my heart because I was still unsettled about the anointing on her life. Caitlyn was going to be a life-changer, but I did not know how. She never had a loud presence. Caitlyn was a behind-the-scenes person. It pained her to be recognized for anything. But I was told Caitlyn was going to do something big for God. Imagine my surprise when Caitlyn told me in her senior year of high school, one month before she was ready to defend her senior thesis, that she was struggling with her faith. We were driving back from soccer practice. She was a phenomenal soccer player, but she had surpassed her performance in her previous years.

I loved watching her play. I went to all her games, even on the rainy, cold days. She was thriving academically, and I was grateful for the few teachers who came alongside her. Caitlyn did not want to be at Trinity because she felt she never fit in. The school was too academic for Caitlyn. She never perceived herself to be an academic scholar. One of the assistant headmasters at the time took Caitlyn under her wing. She helped Caitlyn understand she had different learning styles. This was an eye-opener for Caitlyn, and things shifted. Because she was on a different academic track, Caitlyn needed certain classes that Trinity did not offer in order to get accepted into James Madison University. This administrator started a new advanced science class just for Caitlyn. The science teacher mentored Caitlyn. Because of two outstanding educators, my daughter evolved into a more confident student. Caitlyn had so much going for her during her senior year. It was her best year. One of the teachers editing her senior thesis told me Caitlyn was one of the most gifted writers in her senior class. To be honest, I was a bit surprised. He encouraged me to read her thesis. I was pleasantly surprised by her exceptional writing skills. I encouraged Caitlyn with the teacher's words. She did not believe me. Then she received her paper, and she had gotten one of the highest grades in the class. Sadly, her peers were surprised she had scored higher than them. They made her feel inferior, and it robbed her of the little confidence she had. Caitlyn was initially waitlisted at JMU but was accepted a few months later. Mark and I were far more excited than she was, though we knew she was relieved. I share all this to shed light on my disbelief that Caitlyn doubted God during her best year. People usually struggled with their faith when life turned sour.

I could not believe the young girl who constantly preached to our Muslim neighbor about Jesus questioned God. Whenever my friend was facing a bleak matter, she asked Caitlyn to pray for her. At the young age of five years old, Caitlyn prayed with strong faith. But on that afternoon, Caitlyn said, "Mom, I am going to tell you something, but please don't get mad." Once again, my heart sank, but this time I was driving. We had not told Caitlyn yet about Danielle's issue. My mind was racing. *Caitlyn too?* I was calm. Mark taught me to remain calm. He wanted the girls to feel safe with us. She immediately felt at ease and spoke evenly. Caitlyn was not excitable. She said, "Mom, would you be mad if I told you I don't believe in God?"

I was not prepared for that, but somehow, I responded, "No, Caitlyn I would never be mad about that because even if you do not believe, God believes in you." Though her words rattled me, I was at peace. I heard a soft inner voice say, "Trust Me. This is not the end of her story." I knew the months ahead were going to be long and difficult. I was struggling with how Caitlyn was going to finish Trinity and defend her thesis. We already violated one of the rules and allowed her to get a small tattoo on her neck. I was choosing my battles, and though I did not like tattoos, I knew she was going to get one regardless. I preferred to go with her. It was a small tattoo lettering the words "God is greater than the highs and lows." But I was not going to throw that in her face. She did not need a sermon. She needed unconditional love. She was reading my facial expression, searching for disapproval, but thankfully, I maintained my composure. My family was already juggling a lot, and things were tough.

Her next question stupefied me. She asked, "Mom, do I remind you of John?"

I never told Caitlyn about the calling on her life until then. I also shared John's words with her. "John thought you were most like him, Caitlyn. He said you would encounter tough times but would overcome them. He said you had a heart for the helpless. Like him, he knew you would never label people. You would meet them where they were with the love of Christ."

Caitlyn looked out the window and was quiet. She broke the silence. "Mommy, I am sorry I don't understand God. There is so much about Him I don't understand. I pray hard but can't

185

feel Him. And I don't want to pretend." I told her it was healthy for her to doubt God and that she needed to be honest about it, even if it meant she would fail her thesis. She was staggered by my words. My girls knew I was a people pleaser. But at that moment I was stripped of that stronghold because my daughter needed to hear those words. I told her it was more important to me that she owned her faith, even if it meant she would stray first. Caitlyn was comforted, but my aching heart sought refuge in God's promise. It was rare for me to find comfort in God's promises, but I did for this particular trial. Yes, it was a trial because the months that followed were wearisome.

Caitlyn defended her thesis. She was authentic about her struggle with faith, and she was commended for her honesty. This surprised her, but it also empowered Caitlyn to be transparent. No matter how much trouble she got into, she painstakingly confessed it. Caitlyn made a few wrong choices at the prom after-party and got caught. She was not the only one, but she refused to expose her friends. She bore the blame with great shame. Mark and I were disappointed but were proud of her uprightness. We talked through it with her. As an employee at Trinity, it was difficult to face some parents, but I no longer carried the burden of trying to look good. It was more important to guide my daughter to the right path. Caitlyn was humble, vulnerable, and honest. Those characteristic traits were valuable, and I was not going to let anyone strip her of them. Above all, she was genuinely remorseful. But I knew we had a long road ahead of us. She got into more trouble over the summer before she left for JMU.

Mark was away on a business trip. Caitlyn did not have the heart to tell me what happened. Instead she bore her heart to Danielle. Danielle comforted her but advised her to tell me. She was scared. Caitlyn cried all night over the awful incident. The word got out, and students and parents from Trinity heard about it. Caitlyn was not concerned about their judgment. She was weary and could not carry the burden alone. Danielle walked her down the stairs to the kitchen where I was standing behind the counter. Caitlyn was not ready to share, but Danielle spoke, "Mom, Caitlyn has something to tell you." Caitlyn was pale. Her eyes were swollen, and she was shaking. I quickly grabbed the counter and reminded myself to remain calm. I kept hearing Mark saying, "Always remain calm so they feel safe." For the next twenty minutes, Caitlyn spoke and told me everything. I am not sure how I remained calm, but I did. She was sobbing, and I knew she was genuinely remorseful. She was sad. She was heartbroken. After she finished speaking, I walked over to her, hugged her, and told her everything was going to be fine.

She kept telling me I could punish her, take her phone away, take her car away, or confine her to her room all summer, and I kept responding, "It's okay, Caitlyn. You punished yourself enough. It is over. You are free. It is finished." She then begged me to not tell Mark. She was too ashamed and did not want to hurt him. The girls learned at that point that I was never going to keep anything from their father. She was terrified. I told her I was going to give her time to tell him when he returned. I gave her up to two weeks. Then I would tell him. I was worried about Mark. I knew he would respond well, but I did not want him to be shocked, so I alerted him. I did not share details but told him Caitlyn got into trouble. As expected, he responded lovingly. He, too, felt her remorse. An hour after Caitlyn told me everything, I was receiving phone calls and text messages from some Trinity parents. I no longer had the desire to please or appease, so I was forward with them. I told them that Caitlyn had come forward and that we were working through it. They were stunned that Caitlyn had the courage to be transparent and vulnerable. Some started to question me about their own kids. I told them I would never betray my daughter's trust. I encouraged them to build trusting relationships with their kids.

Caitlyn joined her sister at JMU, refused to participate in any Christian organization, and dived into the party scene. Before she left for college, I told Caitlyn I knew she would party hard, drink too much, and probably get into more trouble. I was not naïve and knew my daughter well. I explained I was not happy about it and hoped she would make good choices. I advised her that she should not accept drinks or rides from anyone or be alone with people. And the dark journey began. I knew we had a long freshman year ahead of us, and I barely slept. I woke up in the middle of the night and would literally get on my knees and pray for Caitlyn. I kept my cell phone on my nightstand and texted her each night to make sure she was back in her dorm safely. She always responded. Danielle was getting frustrated with her, and I advised Danielle to give her space. I wanted Caitlyn to have her own experience. Things got considerably worse, and I was scared. I still had peace, but it was too deep down for me to dip into it. I covered Caitlyn in prayer with Ephesians 3:20. God is able to do more than I expect. He will exceed my expectations. But how? Well, I quickly learned that I did not need to know how. I just needed to trust. When Mark and I visited the girls at JMU, I knew Caitlyn was hung over. I did not beat around the bush and asked her directly. She did not even try to deny it. I knew I needed to pray more. Mark and I even started to pray together because the battle was that intense. A few months passed, and Danielle called to tell me she had to go rescue Caitlyn. Danielle received a call from a friend who was concerned about Caitlyn. Danielle carried Caitlyn back to her place from the party. She bathed her, changed her, and put her to bed with her. Caitlyn woke up the next morning and told Danielle, "No more. I don't want this anymore. Dad worked too hard to save up for my college, and I am squandering his money." And that was the turning point for Caitlyn. She walked away from the party scene, joined Young Life, and studied hard. God certainly exceeded my expectations because I was prepared for a much longer battle. Caitlyn struggled with her faith, searched for answers, but finally owned it. She became a Young Life leader and ministered to high school girls like herself. She woke up at dawn, drove an hour, and spent time with these broken girls. This was where she and John were similar. They looked at these broken people and told them, "I was once like you but found hope in Christ." During her struggles as our family situation intensified, Caitlyn had no one except God. Danielle had her outlet with that sweet counselor, but Caitlyn felt alone. She was not alone because she threw herself into the arms of Jesus and found comfort and joy in His presence. She went to Zambia on a missionary trip with strangers and experienced God in a fresh way. This now was the beginning of a new chapter in Caitlyn's life, one that is still being authored.

Chapter 19
My Stark Journey

A S YOU HAVE READ THROUGHOUT the book, life was challenging, and there were a few hurdles to overcome. My father's sudden death in 1988 was my first tragedy. John's ten-year battle with addiction was daunting. Then his death taxed me. Danielle's pain was unbearable. It broke my heart to watch my daughter suffer. Caitlyn's struggles were debilitating. I was emotionally drained, and my physical deterioration contributed more to my decline. I did not write too much about my health struggle with ulcerative colitis. I was diagnosed—or misdiagnosed—when I was twenty-seven years old and pregnant with Caitlyn in 1997. I was bleeding badly and thought I was having a miscarriage. I was officially diagnosed with this autoimmune disease a few years later. The flare-ups were accompanied with excruciating pain. But despite these oppressive issues, I pushed through. I refused to plummet. Nothing was going to take me down.

My family was struggling, and the reasons are too sensitive to share in this book. I am not ashamed of them, but there is prudence in not divulging all the details. Nonetheless, they became part of the burden. All the other issues were detectable, though not easy to endure. But in the end, they were exposed and dealt with. My strongholds were not detectable until I began to write this book. Since this undertaking, I have been quickly spiraling downhill, but I did not feel it. I never felt it because I always had everything under control. Even when faced with the toughest struggles, including the ones I mentioned with my father, brother, daughters, and health, I still had control over every situation. Every experience taught me a life lesson. But there were a few tougher ones that refined me. I honestly thought I had had enough. While coping with John's death and struggling to raise my daughters, I fell into the trap of the American dream. I was ensnared by materialism. I wanted to live in a mansion, drive luxurious cars, and maintain a wealthy lifestyle—all on one salary. It crept up on me because I definitely did not grow up with a silver spoon in my mouth. We lived modestly. I vehemently pursued my dream, and Mark went along to avoid confrontations. He was far more financially conservative than me because he handled our family finances. I never paid much attention to the numbers, but I wanted Mark to make them work. It was April 2010, and we spent an entire weekend getting our townhouse ready to sell only to make an offer on a house we could not afford. I wanted a specific house in Clifton, Virginia, so badly I wrote a letter to the owners, begging them to lower the price. It was absurd how desperate I was. I felt God should compensate me for my losses. I know now that I was delusional because God did not owe me anything. The Lord loved me too much to leave me in that condition.

After the weekend Mark was supposed to travel for work, so we decided to not list the house until he returned. In the meantime, I took the girls to Danielle's soccer practice, and despite Caitlyn's pleadings to stay home alone, I took her too. During practice I watched twenty fire trucks speed by the fields, and I knew there was a terrible fire nearby. When practice was over, Mark called me frantically. A friend called Mark from the neighborhood across the street from ours to notify him there was a fire in our community. Oddly, Mark went to the wrong airport. He frequently traveled for business and never went to the wrong airport. So he missed his flight and was on his way home. I sped home and was stopped at the opening of our development. The police barricaded our neighborhood and told me to walk home. As the girls and I approached our street, we saw the blazing fire. It was our row of townhouses, but it had started with the opposite end unit. So many emotions ran through my mind, but the one that paralyzed me was losing John's photo albums. My mother and I had argued over keeping John's albums and other belongings. She reluctantly gave in to me, and her exact words were, "What if you lose them in a fire?" As her words taunted me, I begged a fireman to let me into the house. We were the fifth house, and the fire was at the second house. The gas lines were behind our homes, and Washington Gas delayed their arrival so the firemen could not put the fire out. The fire was moving rapidly from attic to attic. John's things were in my attic. I also remembered our cat was in the house. The fireman thought I was insane. I was insufferable, so he escorted me into the house. He was more concerned about the cat and spent most of his time searching for her with no luck. He and I tried to get into the attic, but it was too hot. He was concerned we would get burned or suffer severe heat exhaustion. He literally dragged me out of the house and told me to sit and pray. It turned out he was a strong believer. My Muslim neighbor was hysterical. She saw me praying and asked me if I was talking to Jesus. She sat with me and asked if I thought Jesus could save my house. My cell phone rang. A friend from Trinity Christian School was watching the fire on the news. She called to tell me she saw a guardian angel on the roof of my house. She promised nothing would happen to my house. After she hung up, I looked at my neighbor and told her I believed Jesus would protect my home. Mark finally arrived, and we sat and watched the fire for five hours. Every half hour a house burned. A Lexus exploded in one of the garages, and a dog died. As the fire approached my neighbor's house, I started to doubt God. The firemen could not put the fire out. My neighbor grew more hysterical, and in her despair, she squeezed my arm and yelled, "Tell your Jesus to save my home."

I wanted to pray for her, but I was crippled with fear over losing John's things. My mother was in Egypt, and I did not know how to break the news to her. My neighbor squeezed my arm tighter, and as she cried out, the firemen broke her windows with their hoses. She got on her knees and wept. I fumbled for words, but I assured her the house would not burn. Sure enough, the fire barely made into her attic. The firemen finally put out the fire. She only had water damage. My house was untouched. We only had smoke damage. The fireman walked over to me with a big smile. "Caroline, it was like God put His hand up and protected your home. It was like an angel was watching over your home." I never told him what my friend said. I knew at that moment that Jesus protected my home. My neighbor was relieved until she realized my home was the only one untouched. "Caroline, your Jesus protected your home."

My family moved into a hotel for a few months. Though we only had smoke damage, the insurance company renovated the house and made it look brand new. In the meantime, we loved hotel living. Trinity Christian School provided dinner daily for the months we stayed in the hotel. The insurance company covered all our expenses. After we moved back home, our house sold immediately. We were not expecting a quick sale, so we temporarily moved into a condo in Fairfax. We planned to live there for one month, hoping to find a permanent residence. I enjoyed condo living more than I expected and delayed searching for a house. I even hosted school parties. The amenities were wonderful, and the complex was like a resort. Our unit overlooked the pool, and we enjoyed the serene view. I had no desire to move out. Six months passed, and the girls were tired of sharing a bedroom. I started to think about it, but then I was hospitalized. I contracted Clostridium difficile (Cdiff) and was hospitalized for two weeks. I had never been so sick in my life. My entire colon was bleeding out, and I suffered unbearable pain. It was worse than my two C-sections. I lost twenty pounds and looked frail. Because of the extensive damage it did to my colon, I was prescribed an IV medication and other strong medications for life. The side effects were horrific, and at times I thought I was losing my mind.

This ordeal delayed us another month. After I was released from the hospital, summer was almost over, and the girls were getting ready to return to school. I also started the IV treatments, and it took time for my body to adjust to this foreign invasion. I was weak and depleted of energy, but I knew we could not stay much longer in the condo. I grew so much during those months and was no longer consumed with materialism. My desires changed. I struggled to leave condo living. It exceeded my expectations, and I learned the valuable lesson of not needing much to be happy.

One afternoon the girls and I were out and drove by the home we ended up purchasing. We stumbled upon it accidentally. We followed the "For Sale" sign, and the owners reluctantly allowed us to tour the home without an agent. The house was not well kept, but I looked past the mess and loved the home. The location was also ideal. I realized I would never have survived living in Clifton on five acres with no neighbor in sight. I needed people. The neighborhood in Clifton was beautiful, but I was an urban girl who enjoyed walking to coffeehouses and shops. Mark was surprised when he toured the home later. It was different than all the mansions I thought I loved. We made an offer, and it was rejected. Mark almost made a higher offer, but we agreed to not budge. Instead we went on vacation with the girls. When we returned, our offer was accepted, and we moved into our new home. It was better than anything I dreamed of. I never needed a mansion or five acres to be happy. My home was still big, but that was not the issue. My deeply rooted issue was a heart issue. If it wasn't for the fire, I would not have been transformed. Since then, materialism never fulfilled me. Don't get me wrong. I enjoy the luxuries of life, but they don't complete me. The house fire was a tough lesson, but it was a blessing.

Chapter 20
How?

T HE ONE QUESTION THAT PUZZLED me about John's life was *how.* How did John experience God the way he did? How did God redeem John from the pit after ten long years? How did God use John's good, bad, and ugly and make them so beautiful? How did John have hope when his situation deemed hopeless? I desperately wanted to publish this book just to fulfill the promise I made to John. Something was holding me back. I could not sell something I did not experience or believe in my heart. Regardless of how superficial I could be, I could not pretend. I no longer pursued a pretentious lifestyle; it depleted me of all my energy. I wanted to understand hope but realized my heart was hardened. Much to my dismay, I rejected God and refused to let Him into my heart.

Despite my tumultuous journey through life, I was stubborn and would not surrender. It took years until I finally came to the end of myself, and it was horrible, to say the least. I came face-to-face with trials and tribulations I could not endure. I lost myself in the shuffle and was no longer the strong, controlled woman I thought I was. My family crumbled. My health deteriorated tremendously, and I lost my mind in between. Life came at me full force, and I felt like a punching bag. I was being punched by betrayal, abandonment, chronic illness, lack of faith, broken relationships, grief, agony, and unbearable sufferings. I had emotional outbursts, and I was not prepared to deal with the aftermath. The medications treating my autoimmune disease took a toll on my mind and body. My body was growing weaker, and the colitis was wreaking havoc on my colon. I was in constant physical pain in addition to emotional and mental anguish. Even when doctors recommended antidepressants to offset the side effects of my colitis medications, I refused. I thought I could handle the side effects on my own. Yet despite these struggles, I was too proud to seek help. Instead I pushed myself harder.

I was losing hope but could never utter such words because I was a Christian who tried to believe. I preached Christ to people. I told people to read the Bible and go to church. I was standing at the crossways and pointing people in the right direction. But sadly, I did not follow. Anger, bitterness, and resentment took root in my heart. My pain was deep. My silent cry for help was stifled, yet I could not contain it much longer. Just like John, I came to the end of myself. It took John ten long years, and admittedly, it took me longer. I lost hope because I isolated myself and tried to do it on my own. I lost hope in God and in myself. I fell into despair and could not find my way out. I never envisioned my life would take such a turn but it did. I failed to dip into the power of God because I was stubbornly trying to be my own God. I foolishly thought I saved John and could save myself. Yet God pursued me inexorably. He had a bigger plan for this book and would not let me escape His mission. The Lord came alongside me to finish writing one of the greatest stories ever told. While I thought I was only writing about my brother's triumph, it was also about me finding hope in Christ, and I lived to tell about it. Because God wanted to use me effectively, He permitted daunting times to strengthen my faith. I was not prepared for the challenging path He chose for me. I would have devised a different plan, but I quickly learned His ways were not my ways and His thoughts were not my thoughts. I never expected to fall. I thought I was too strong for God. Well, I was wrong, my friends. I fell, and the plummet was so long, hard, and deep, I often wondered if even God could reach me.

It was the winter of 2016, and life was bitter. A surge of indignant emotions washed over me and left me in despair. I was angry, sad, lost, and hopeless. I attended church weekly but regressed further in my spiritual development. I read the Bible daily, but the words had no bearing on me. I lost trust in God, people, and myself. I felt so much, and I felt nothing. One night my sufferings consumed me, and I made imprudent choices. As a result, I went into a dark place in my mind. The worst place to get lost was in my head. I could not find my way out. My tongue knew no boundaries and unleashed thirty years of stored-up, embittered emotions. It was my dark and stormy night, one I wish I could erase from my story. I reluctantly included it here, but it was a pivotal chapter in my story. I felt ashamed but was pressed to embrace it because it was part of a bigger plan, not my plan but God's plan.

Danielle called 911. She and my mother were with me in the car and knew I was in serious trouble. Soon we were surrounded by sirens, and the loud piercing sounds exasperated my condition. I would not let anyone touch me, but one officer was finally able to hold me in his arms. My vision was blurred, and my speech was slurred. "Officer, can you please take your gun and shoot me? I killed my baby." The gruesome images of the abortion I had undergone shortly before my wedding invaded my mind. I constantly saw myself slaying my baby. Because I left no room for God to rule over me, I judged and condemned myself. I kept seeing images of a baby boy. I'd always felt the baby was a boy. I wanted to hold him so badly, but he was too far out of my reach. I aborted my baby because I feared people's judgments. Though Mark encouraged me to confess with him, I never repented. I never mourned the loss. I never dealt with this pain. When the graphic images flooded my mind that night, I felt great remorse. The anguish was intense. I never regretted anything in my life more than the abortion. I spent years after Danielle and Caitlyn trying to conceive a son, but every attempt failed. There was no logical explanation why Mark and I could not conceive again. I got pregnant with Danielle while I was on birth control. Then we had Caitlyn two years later. My desire for a son burned within me, and I begged God for a baby. I thought I was being punished for the abortion. God was not punishing me. He gave Mark and me two amazing daughters. I finally prayed the desire away, so the Lord eventually removed it from my heart. And though it reappeared on that dreadful night, it was only to bring me to repentance and to have closure. A few years after this night, a pastor prayed with me to receive God's love. Though it took years, I finally accepted God's forgiveness. The pastor's words comforted me. "Caroline, your baby is not dead. He is waiting for you in heaven." I forgave myself and grieve with hope. Even until today, I can't talk about it without sobbing. The abortion was one of my deepest sufferings, but it was not the only one.

I was hospitalized immediately, and my condition deteriorated rapidly. The doctors were concerned about my physical ailments and a mixture of medications. Unfortunately, my injudicious choices throughout the evening contributed to the harsh effects the medications were having on my mind and body. I was in and out of consciousness. The same officer who held me earlier was by my bedside, stroking my hair. I kept hearing his kind and gentle voice whispering in my ear, "Everything will be fine." It was as if my father was with me. I tuned out every sound in the hospital room except for his voice. Those were the last words I heard before I blacked out completely.

A few days prior to that dreadful night, I was with my daughters at Rockefeller Center in New York City to see the Christmas tree. As we walked, explored, and ventured through New York, I keenly observed the way people were preparing for Christmas. I recalled John's words about experiencing the true meaning of Christmas. I pondered what it really meant to experience Christmas the way John did. There was an odd but deep longing in my heart to celebrate Christmas with just Jesus and me, no gifts, tree, people, or feast to prepare. God certainly answered that longing or prayer. Honestly, it irked me how God answered some prayers promptly yet waited years to answer other prayers.

I woke up hours later in a foreign bed, a room I did not recognize. I was cold but was covered with a light blanket. There were two other women in the room, but they were sleeping. There was a bathroom in the room with the lights on. I got out of bed and walked outside the room. This young woman approached me. She was dressed in white and had a bedsheet wrapped around her head. She asked me, "Do you believe in Jesus?"

All I kept thinking was, *Did I die and go to heaven?* So I responded, "Yes, of course, I believe in Jesus."

And she said, "Oh, good, because I am Him."

I was not in heaven, but then I thought, *Am I in hell?* The nurse behind the desk asked her to return to her room. As I walked toward the desk, a man touched my hair and told me it was beautiful. I panicked but was more concerned about my whereabouts. After these people were sent to their rooms, the nurse took me into a waiting room and told me everything that had occurred the night before. I was in disbelief. I barely remembered any of the details. He told me a doctor was on his way to talk with me. The doctor was waiting for me to wake up. I asked for my family, and the nurse told me that I had wanted to be left alone. I was sad to learn I had pushed my family away.

The doctor entered the room. He was young but appeared competent. He was of Indian descent, though I thought he looked more Egyptian. He wanted to know how much I remembered, and when he realized that I didn't remember much, we read through the reports together. After we were done, I asked, "Doctor, what is happening to me?"

He looked at me for a few minutes. His eyes were imperturbable. His voice was pacifying, and he replied, "Caroline, you've suffered much trauma in your life. It was too much for one person to handle. It maimed your health." I was deeply concerned when he told me I wanted my life to end. I was always a happy, optimistic, and upbeat person. I was high on life and encouraged people to see the bright side of every situation. Why did I want my life to end? He set aside his medical profession briefly and told me a story of a great man who wanted God to end his life. He shared the story of Elijah from the Bible in order to show me even the great prophet fell into despair. But God tended to his needs and rejuvenated him. I could not accept the correlation between Elijah and me because I felt worthless at that moment. I appreciated the doctor's godly perspective because it somehow put me at ease. I asked him if I should be medicated, but he was opposed to prescribing additional medications. They would further harm my colon. When he learned I was dabbling in trial medications for colitis, he discouraged me. He was confident they were having an adverse effect on my mind. I was exploring other options to heal from my debilitating disease, and I was taking dangerous risks. He maintained his professional demeanor but saw a deep longing within me for spiritual healing. The doctor was a devout Christian and only shared his faith because he knew I was a Christian. He encouraged me to seek Christian counseling to grow strong in my faith. He recognized my faith was shaken, and as we talked through my life—past, present, and future—he pointed me to Jesus Christ. He told me God was my answer, my healer. The doctor did not neglect his medical proficiency. He treated me pathologically first. It was his chief priority to adjust my medications and address the unheeded health issues that curtailed from my infusion treatments.

Then he proceeded to guide me spiritually because he could not neglect my longing for spiritual healing. I did not recall seeking it, but he heard a groaning that came from deep within. His next words were profound, but I did not understand them until a few years later. There was a connection between my spiritual and physical healings. He advised me to seek spiritual healing and promised physical restoration would follow. There was no division between the two realms. Though we don't see the spiritual realm, it does not diminish its existence. It's too complex to write more on this topic, but he was not the first person to mention it. When I was in Africa in 2001, I met privately with a monk and coveted his prayers for healing. I was suffering from chronic flare-ups and needed a miracle. He was a holy man who spent most of his days in solitude praying. People had witnessed his miracles, and they believed he was a saint. In his presence I was at peace, but I was intimidated by his holiness. I felt he could see through me. He spoke with an Australian accent, "Caroline, daughter of the Almighty, I am praying for your spiritual healing because it is of more value than your physical. Your physical sickness is strongly connected to a spiritual illness, so ask the Lord to reveal it and heal it." His words left me unsettled. I struggled to listen. It was not a skill I mastered. He also spoke on a level I did not understand. I misinterpreted his words and basically heard him telling me that God was punishing me for my sins. I mentioned in the foreword that I was in a bad place, so it was easy to feel condemned. I disregarded his words until my conversation with the doctor. I continued to hear the same thing from different people. I thought their faith was charismatic so their words fell on deaf ears. I began to understand it better when my cousin sent me a website about spiritual and physical healings. I researched ulcerative colitis, and it was connected to the spiritual disease of control. That was an eye-opener for me. It helped me better understand my disease, but it took time to fully grasp it. I was not ready to release control yet.

God answered my prayer, and I experienced a different kind of Christmas because of that night. There was no tree, no gifts, no feast but just Jesus and me. Well, to be honest, I did not really feel Jesus's presence yet. I had a misconstrued understanding of God's presence. Jesus was with me, but I expected it to be different. I was sad, hopeless, and ashamed. I could not think. I rested my thoughts because they hurt my head. I yearned for my father and John, seeking their comfort. I wanted my father to tell me that everything was going to be fine. All I had was a UVA student in the bed next to me who clung to me like I was her mother. She experienced terrible trauma and was hospitalized before me. She would not get out of bed. She did not speak to anyone and refused to eat. But for some strange reason, she was drawn to me. She sat up in bed and spoke for the first time in days. I learned everything about her in a half hour. She was a senior at UVA and was already accepted into medical school, but life happened. I listened to her story, and it was gut-wrenching. She had no one to care for her. No one visited her. So I let her visit with my family. They enjoyed meeting her. When my family visited for the first time, I wept. I had no words for them. I did not know what to say to Danielle and Caitlyn. I was their mother, their hero, and I had let them down. I could not face my mother, for whom I had always remained strong. I had failed her too. I had no words for Mark. But they all loved me well.

Jackie called, and I broke down when I heard her voice. We talked for a while. No one knew the extent of my anguish. My mother and Jackie were most surprised because we talked often, but I never unleashed any of my burdens on them. I was the one they leaned on. Jackie was supportive, understanding, loving, and gentle. My spiritual mentor visited and cried with me. She told me the same thing she had been telling me since the beginning. She was the only one who knew the details and not because I told her. One day she felt prompted by the Holy Spirit to visit me. She was obedient to God's Word and came to my home immediately. I was struggling that afternoon, and I asked God to send someone to pray with me. My doorbell rang, and as soon as I saw my friend, I knew our friendship had a greater purpose. Our relationship grew deeper in Christ, and she became a lifetime mentor. Since then, we've been praying together. One of the most valuable lessons she taught me was to not get caught up in details. She assured me that God knew them all. She was only there to point me to Jesus Christ. At the hospital she held my hands and said, "Caroline,

Jesus loves you so much. All you need is Jesus. God has amazing plans for the Guirgis family. Just trust Him." After she left, her profound words stayed with me.

All I need is Jesus, I sadly thought. *Then why isn't Jesus enough?*

The UVA student disrupted my thoughts and said, "Caroline, you have a beautiful family. Your daughters are so pretty. They are lucky to have you as their mother. I could see how much you love your family." She bluntly asked me, "Why is Jesus all you need? Like why is He so important? If He is all you need, then how do you get Him?" My mind searched for the answer. I was still grappling with that question, "If Jesus was all I needed, why was He not enough?" My family brought me my Bible and journal. I pulled out my Bible and told my new friend we were going to read the Christmas story since it was Christmas Eve. I gazed at her and was filled with great compassion for her. She was alone in this world. She had no one to love her. I briefly stopped dwelling on my situation and focused on my new friend. She gleefully jumped out of bed and was motivated to shower for the first time in days.

We got our drinks, snacks, and blankets and went to the community room. We sat in the corner and made a picnic. The television was loud. People were either arguing or talking. It was hard to discern between the two. But she and I were able to create a beautiful, serene, quiet place to read the Christmas story. I opened up with a prayer, and she cried the whole time. She told me that she had never heard anyone pray. The prayer softened her heart, and she relaxed. I had a soft spot for her. She was young, vulnerable, beautiful, smart, and very funny. She made me laugh a lot. After we prayed, we ate all our favorite snacks. We savored each bite and enjoyed the Oreo cookies, graham crackers, Goldfish, and pretzels. After our stomachs were full, I turned to the gospel of Luke in the Bible and started reading. Soon after I started reading, the room grew quiet, and when I looked up, every eye in the room was on me. I initially thought people were mad, but they gathered around to hear the Christmas story. One of the nurses told me this was the first time someone had brought Christmas there. Holidays were not celebrated. It was not politically correct.

As I finished each chapter, they wanted me to read more. Before I knew it, we finished the gospel of Luke. Then one woman ended with singing "Joy to the World." She sang angelically, and everyone chimed in. It was beautiful, absolutely breathtaking. I experienced the real Christmas. Peace, joy, and love were unmatched gifts placed in my heart. I coveted no other gifts, and I had all I needed. I was fulfilled. I was surrounded by strangers who were stripped of hope, dignity, and everything they possessed, yet they found joy in the gospel message. My new friend summed up the evening perfectly when she said, "Jesus Christ is all we need. He is our hope." Christmas cheer filled the room with laughter as people ate and played games. It was my best Christmas. I felt the presence of Jesus. He was there in our midst, loving on His broken people, and I was the chief among them. My friend and I watched *The Sound of Music*. It was her first time seeing it, and she enjoyed it very much. I loved that movie, especially when I watched it with my daughters. But for that night I needed to love this young lady. Such love began to mend my broken spirit.

My young friend was released from the hospital to continue her education. We stayed in touch for a short while. I, too, was discharged and returned home. I was feeble and struggled to navigate through life's hardships. My family was instrumental in guiding me. It was a difficult transition, but I did my best to jump back into life. I was traumatized by the whole ordeal, but it initiated minor inner healing. I was ashamed to face my extended family because I wanted to keep my crisis private, but I felt exposed. They prayed for me and reached out almost daily. One of my cousins entered my mess and stayed in it with me. She constantly called and encouraged me with scripture. It continued to be a challenging year with hurdles I could not overcome. I sought help everywhere and searched for hope in things and people, but nothing fulfilled me. In the meantime, my health condition worsened, and the IV treatment started to work against my body. It did minor damage to my left lung, and I had bronchitis and pneumonia a couple of times within one year. I also had mono, which depleted me of all my energy. I barely got up for work and dozed off periodically throughout the day at my desk.

I had a friend who worked at NYU, and he made me an appointment with a GI specialist. The specialist changed my infusion treatment immediately. The new medication was better since my body did not reject it, but the side effects were the same. I was not healing promptly, so I went against medical advice and tried a new trial medication. I failed to understand the impact it could have on my mind. This one had the worst side effect—cold sweats, nausea, chronic migraines, anxiety, accelerated heart rate, and heightened emotions. I developed migraines daily since I started the trial in June and went until the fall. My head hurt constantly. I started to lose my mind. Most of the time, I was well composed, but I had a few episodes. The one I regretted the most happened at work, and it was a turning point for me. It was still the one area in my life not affected by my decline. It was by design because pride had a tight grip on me. I had been working at Trinity since 2004 and always managed to keep it together, even when John died in 2005. Then in the fall of 2017, I had an emotional meltdown in front of a few of my coworkers. I was disappointed with the way a work situation was handled. It was not a big deal, but in my mind, it was. Nonetheless, I broke down. I could no longer keep it together. The loss of control distressed me. I realized at that point that I needed to get off that medication. Though I wished my meltdown had never happened, some of my coworkers loved me through it. They cared deeply for me, and I was touched by their outreach. As soon as I started to wean off the medication, I started to feel like myself again. I was beating myself up over the incident, but I realized I needed to let go and move on. I no longer felt the need to defend myself, and I prayed for restoration and reconciliation. God answered immediately, and

I was grateful. I was fortunate to have closure, but I knew I needed to make immediate changes to wean off all my medications. My mind did not need the extra stress.

I did not have the motivation, strength, or desire to implement the necessary changes. My body grew weaker, and I was getting sicker after every injection every two weeks. My weakened condition stripped me of the ability to exercise. My workouts were producing endorphins, which were good for my mind, but I was too exhausted to go to the gym. I thought this was my end, especially after the difficult experiences I had encountered. I was stripped of everything. I wanted to relinquish control and surrender. Why couldn't I just let go? Why was I being so stubborn? Despite my stark journey, I continued to socialize, manage my household, maintain friendships, and be present for the family. But it was a struggle. For the first time in my life, people agitated me despite my jovial and extrovert personality. I had a low tolerance for people and noise. For some reason, only the students at work brought me joy. They lifted up my spirits, and I enjoyed being with them eight hours a day. I also had a part-time job at a local boutique. I initially took the job to help pay down my astronomical medical bills. But it became my happy place. I loved fashion and enjoyed helping women accessorize. I knew neither the students nor my part-time job was my hope. As my health deteriorated and my crisis intensified, my spiritual life declined tremendously. I was confronted with hopelessness and despair. The battlefield in my mind became the focal point of my life. My thoughts were toxic, and they poisoned my mind, seeping into my heart as well.

Chapter 21
My God, My Only Hope

Behold, I am doing a new thing: now it springs
forth, do you not perceive it? I will make a way in
the wilderness and rivers in the desert.

—Isaiah 43:19

DANIELLE MOVED BACK HOME AFTER she graduated in 2017. She posted this scripture on our refrigerator. I was grateful God redeemed Danielle. I witnessed the fruits of His labor in her dealings with me and others. For years I felt guilty and struggled to forgive myself. When I received the Mother of the Year Award in May 2016 from Passion for Moms at their annual conference, I could not accept it. When the CEO of the organization announced my name, I froze and envisioned myself in a dark tunnel. I saw Danielle drowning and did not extend my arm to save her. I just watched her. I did not deserve the award. The worship team beautifully sang "This Is My Story" by Big Daddy Weave while a slideshow of my family photos was on display. There were more than five hundred women in the room. The headmaster of Trinity was on stage ready to present me with the award. His assistant and my friend was the one who nominated me. She placed her hand on my shoulder, not knowing my internal struggle. My mother and sister attended the conference for the first time. Jackie gasped and looked at me with admiration and respect. My mother was proud of me. The CEO was a cherished friend who respected me. Yet despite all the admiration and respect, I could not accept the award. Thankfully, the song was long, and as I struggled with my thoughts, God spoke clearly into my heart and said, "You are forgiven. You are free. Receive this award as a gift from Me." I humbly received the award, knowing all the glory was given to God. Every time I read that scripture on my refrigerator, I am reminded of the new thing God did in Danielle and me and the new thing He will continue to do. The Lord was always there.

Throughout my journey God placed certain people on my path at the right moment. I was fortunate to have prayer warriors on my side. Even when I could not pray, these women carried me. Every day someone sent me scriptures either by text or email. Some of them even committed to praying for this book. They know who they are, and I know God will bless them abundantly for pointing me to Him. They continue to pour into me today. I am blessed to have them in my life. Social media became another source of encouragement for me. I was able to filter through it and read empowering spiritual words. There was a pastor I met on Facebook through a mutual friend. His posts redirected me to Jesus daily, and I was encouraged by them. The one that resonated with me was dated December 2017. I was coming to end of myself, but Pastor Jose Miranda's words were impactful.

> If you're going through a difficult time in your life right now, I want to encourage you with these words. You're not alone. I know that it seems that there's no sunlight in your day right now. But this will pass. Please do not get bitter. Choose to forgive. Easier said than done. I know that. However, you have to ask God to give you strength, and He will! There are many things that you may not understand at this moment. But you

will look back in the near future and understand that this difficulty has only made you stronger, wiser, and better. The Lord is your strength and your Hightower. He is your place of Refuge. Trust in the Lord with all of your heart. Even when things don't make sense. It is okay to cry. Because God understands how you feel. But do not park your life in a ditch of despair. You will come out of this. You will come out of this strong! I speak life to you right now in the name of Jesus! Your best days are not behind you, they are right in front of you! I declare that you will rise up and accomplish the purposes of God for your life. You are needed! Believe it or not, you are someone else's miracle. Do not cut your life short by believing the lies inside of your mind. You were born to win! And you were created for greatness! Be encouraged today and know that you are loved and not alone! Nothing is too difficult for our God. Even in the midst of a negative report, you will NOT BE SHAKEN! Let God arise mightily in you and every enemy be scattered! You will come out of this Victorious! Speak life. Speak faith. Speak His Word!

God's timing was perfect. He wanted to show me things as He prepared my heart to see His wonderful works. I was always an optimistic person, but through these trials, I lost the ability see good and have a positive attitude. The Lord wanted to give me something better than optimism. He wanted to give me hope. Hope is believing in the unseen. It's having unwavering faith despite harsh circumstances. God answered a prayer I prayed a few years ago. It was the last heartfelt prayer I uttered. It was New Year's Eve 2015, and things were bad. I was driving alone on Route 66, and anger engulfed me. For the first time, I cursed at God. There were times I had doubts and wavered in my faith, but I never cursed God. It was startling, and I deserved to be punished. I thought God would stop protecting me from an accident and let me burn in hell. I was appalled by my behavior. Instead of experiencing the wrath of God, I experienced His vast love. I pulled my car over. I felt great warmth and a sense of peace I did not understand, I was confused. I wanted God to punish me, but He wanted to love me. As I settled down, I prayed, "Lord, please give me unwavering faith. I never want my faith to be shaken. No matter what I face in life, I want you to be my hope." Dr. Peter Teague defined faith perfectly when he said, "Faith is seeing the impossible, knowing the unknowable, and believing the unbelievable, so that we may achieve the impossible." I coveted such faith. Oh, boy! I had no idea what I had just done. The Lord was faithful and answered my prayer. God does not punish, but He does discipline out of love and mercy.

In Christ, I knew who I was; however, through my circumstances I discovered my true identity, and it was not a pretty image. But just like John, God did not want me to lose myself in my crisis. I wanted God to be my safe haven. Just as I prayed scripture over my daughters, people did the same for me. Amazingly, one specific verse became the one for me. These women came from different walks of my life and were not acquainted with one another. Yet they sent me the same verse. "The Lord your God is with you, He is mighty to save. He will take great delight in you, He will quiet you with His love, He will rejoice over you with singing" (Zephaniah 3:17).

Yes! I needed to be quiet because I talked too much. I had an answer for everything, but God wanted to quiet me with His love. This was hard for someone like me. As I practiced silence, I spent more time with the Lord. I listened to praise music and meditated on His Word daily. He rejoiced over me with His singing. Though I was lonely, I was not alone because God showed up. The Holy Spirit ministered to me and walked me through my trials. He showed me each one had a purpose to purify me and draw me nearer to Him. I was crying out to people to save me, but it was God who removed them from my path so that He could move in. I felt abandoned by some people, especially pastors and priests, but Jesus wanted to be my highest priest.

As 2017 was coming to an end and I was editing this book one last time, I slowly relinquished control. As I started to let go, the Lord helped me finish writing because I could not do it. I became an instrument in His hand and obeyed His instructions. I did not want to include my shameful encounters, but I realized that they were part of my story and that He was the author. I was no longer embarrassed by them. But I was fatigued. Even though I was weary, the Lord still wanted me to serve Him. He poured His love into me and gave me the strength to serve people's needs. He placed people in my path. I did not feel worthy of such a calling, but I obeyed God. He was transforming me through my ministry to others. His strength was perfected in my weakness. He renewed my strength as I submitted to Him. As I continued to pray for others, my daughters became my strongest prayer warriors. I was humbled by their spiritual depth and insight. Caitlyn imparted these words on me: "Mom, you are so valued and cherished. There is a throne in heaven with your name on it. You are a child of God and nothing and no one can ever change that. Everything on earth is temporary, but our heavenly throne remains. Don't ever stop looking up to that throne and to our Father for peace and joy in everything!" Her words reminded me of C. S. Lewis's words, which John once quoted, "Aim at heaven and you will get earth thrown in. Aim at earth and you get neither." The Lord quieted me with His love through my daughter.

I responded to Caitlyn and said, "I don't know what to say, Caitlyn, but thank you."

She replied, "No, Mommy, thank you. You are the reason I am able to speak these words into your life today. You are reaping what you have sown in me." I was speechless. I was humbled. But

I knew it was not me. It was God. It was all Him. His grace met my daughters in their darkness, and He became their light and hope. And I was grateful. Danielle shared a quote by Lisa Harper she recently learned. "Gratitude is the soil where obedience and humility grow."

Finally, the question I had been asking all these years was answered on New Year's Day 2018. It only took thirteen years, but it was worth the wait. "How do I have hope in the midst of my sufferings?" On New Year's Eve, I ran into my spiritual mentor by chance. It was not planned. She told me she had a vision of me in church that morning when she was praying for me. She saw the Lord place a shield on my chest to protect me. She placed her hands on my shoulders and looked into my eyes. "Caroline, your breakthrough is coming this year. The Lord has amazing plans for the Guirgis family. Just wait and see." I knew those were God's Words because I totally surrendered at that moment. I let go of everything and rested in Christ. I was in awe of what I had experienced. I was in a public setting but retreated to a quiet place to be in the presence of Jesus. I loved my friend dearly, and she has been a great source of comfort through it all. But I needed Jesus! In the past I would have expected all my circumstances to vanish and my sufferings to dissipate so I could live with hope. I wished that so badly. But I knew that was not the case. In His presence, the Lord revealed to me that He wanted me to have hope while I was still suffering. This was difficult, but He was with me. Things were rough through the night into the next day, but I kept my eyes on Jesus. Just as God is real, so is Satan. There was a battle in the spiritual realm, and the devil was not going to sit back and let me surrender to God.

He became a stumbling block, and I fell. But the Lord was with me. As I came face-to-face with my crisis that morning, I was getting weak, but I felt God's strength. Jesus was with me, and I kept my eyes on Him. My focus shifted, and I kept going back and forth. I would take my eyes off Him and set my gaze upon my circumstance while words were spewed at me. The Lord spoke and said, "Do not receive these words. They are not Mine. Keep your eyes on Me. Look at Me. I am with you." I couldn't look at Him because I believed the lies. It was easier to surrender to my circumstances. I was losing hope. I was terrified. I was confused. I was a woman of words but had none to speak. The words people spoke into my life came to fruition, and I was surrounded by an army of God's people. I saw the Lord place a beautiful bedazzled breastplate on my chest. I felt the arms of Jesus around me. The Lord embraced me, and I melted into His arms. I took my eyes off everyone, every circumstance, every suffering and looked to Jesus. The storms of life waved over me but never washed me away because Jesus was in the storm with me. "I will personally go with you, and I will give you rest—everything will be fine for you" (Exodus 33:14).

My daddy was right when he said, "Everything will be fine." My crisis was not averted, but I am resting in Jesus's arms. Though I am still walking through the valley of the shadow of death, I will no longer fear evil because the Lord is with me. I am only *walking* through my circumstances. I am not staying there. Whether my circumstances change or not, my hope is in Christ alone. As I wait on God, I take great comfort in His promise, which says, "When the time is right, I, the Lord will make it happen" (Isaiah 60:22).

I came to the end of myself, which was the best place to be. Now I am on a new journey. It is the beginning of my renewed life with Christ Jesus, my God, my only hope!

Chapter 22
The Roaring R's

GOD REDEEMED, RESTORED, AND RENEWED John. It was loud like a lion's roar. No person had the power to thwart God's plan. It ushered John into God's glorious kingdom, where he celebrates victory for eternity. John's life spoke volumes, and many were saved. He was not ashamed to share his past. It was a place of reference, not refuge because John never settled there. He was like a city on a hill and was not ashamed to proclaim the gospel that saved him. John was salt and light. He seasoned people's lives to preserve their faith in God. His presence was bright, and people walked from darkness into light. He did not hide behind his addiction. He surrendered it to God, and the Lord bequeathed him the greatest gift, Himself.

I was honored John chose me to write his story. It was the most daunting undertaking, but it was worth it. The thirteen-year journey exceeded my expectations and transformed my life. I would not have chosen this path for myself. But I am grateful I don't have such authority. As I surrendered to God, I valued His sovereignty and rested in His wisdom. I matured through my trials and learned valuable lessons. My trials were harsh, and I irrationally reacted to my circumstances. My situations changed daily, but God's love was steadfast. He transformed my mind to respond to Him and not react to my disappointments. This was a tough lesson because it took years of suffering to overcome my weakness. Like John, I tried to do it on my own. I was never alone because the Holy Spirit dwells within me. God is always near. He fashioned life lessons for me and gave me new eyes to see the blessings that arose from them. Whenever I questioned God, He answered, "Ask me what blessing am I receiving through this trial?" I was asking the wrong questions. There was nothing wrong with crying out to God. Job did. He was always my point of reference because of the sufferings he endured. But when Job came face-to-face with God, his questions dissipated. He received more than what he lost. John never considered his ten years of addiction a loss because he gained eternity. I no longer consider these past thirteen years a loss. I look to eternity as a greater gain.

Jesus Christ has the power to redeem anyone, especially you! No one is too far gone for His reach. He already won your battle and set you free from Satan's grip. Take courage and fight your battle from a position of victory. He heals your pain and eases your sufferings. Trusting the Lord without fear brings hope to any hopeless situation. No matter what you are facing, persevere with faith. "Don't be afraid; just believe" (Mark 5:36).

Don't deceive yourself into thinking you don't have faith. You do believe. You believe that when you sit in a chair, it will hold you. You believe that when you order your meal, you will get it. You believe that when you work, you will get paid. You believe that if you work hard, you will succeed. You believe that when you turn on your car, it will start. You do have faith, but it may be misplaced.

Jesus Christ died for everyone and invites all to receive His love. Don't judge Him because of the way people treat you. God is greater than people. People label you with the mark of your sin, but Jesus removes the label. He knows your sin and loves you unconditionally. Because He loves you, He desires for you to confess and repent of your sins. Through the Holy Spirit, He renews your life and gives you fresh eyes to see the wonderful life He planned for you. His love is genuine, and it binds broken hearts.

He desires to enter your heart and guide you through this fleeting life. This world is temporary, and it will perish. But His kingdom is everlasting. Choose Jesus Christ and follow Him today. Open your heart and receive Christ as your Savior. He is the only way! I don't have all the answers, but I'm willing to share my journey with you. I encourage you to visit my blog at http://carolineguirgis. wordpress.com. It is a compilation of lessons I learned and grew from. The life lessons evolved into blessings, and I want to share them with you.

If you wish to be part of the gift that keeps on giving, please share this book with someone who needs to bind their mind to the Mind of Christ. It starts with one person and today, that is you. Help me spread this message of Hope. Together we become new creations in Christ the Lord and make a radical difference in today's society.

You may also donate to the John Hanna Foundation and help others overcome their struggles. I may be reached at guirgisc@ yahoo.com for donations but more importantly to pray for you and with you.

The Alpha and Omega

The Beginning Starts at the End was written to share the hope my brother found in Jesus Christ. This book does not deny the teachings of any doctrines or dogmas. It is not a book on theology or religion. John and my father taught me all who follow Jesus Christ are part of one family. We are not divided by denominations because we are united in the body of Christ. It is my earnest plea that all followers of Christ are united. Together, we can conquer the world and spread the message of love. Hurt people hurt people, but love binds and heals every wound. May we become like a city on a hill and proclaim the gospel with *love*. When we look to Jesus Christ, we will radiate His love, and every knee will bow before Him. This book was written out of love. May you receive it with love! "I am the Alpha and the Omega, the first and the last, the beginning and the end" (Revelation 22:13). Marantha!

"Well done, good and faithful servent; enter into the joy of your master."
- Matthew 25:21

John's favorite photo

Printed in the United States
By Bookmasters